Manchester Eve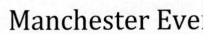

By

Norman Beaker

PREFACE

This book is not so much a personal biography as a very public one, lived out in different settings and over far too many decades to contemplate.

Many times, I have been asked to put down in writing some of the trials, tribulations, and funny things that have happened to me along the way, and so here we are due to public demand the Biography of a Manchester Blues Guitarist. '**The Manchester Evening Blues** '

Although the contents are from my own memory bank which I presume will soon start to decline or crash, they are for everybody else's amusement and mostly at my expense.

When I first started to play guitar, I had no ambition to be a pop star even if I had been given better looks than God dished up, but I did have an incredible urge to learn to play.

As I progressed my goals changed, and I decided that I would be more than happy if I just got to play with some of my heroes. Thankfully with only a few exceptions, where I have been cheated by their premature demise, I have succeeded.

It seems to be the way of the world that when one's ambitions are met, that they fail to live up to expectations, I can honestly say that has never been the case with the people I have been lucky enough to have performed with. They have all left a lasting impression on me and have been some of the greatest teachers anyone could have wished for.

As the book is about my exploits, it will of course be necessary to include snippets about my upbringing, but I will keep these down to the minimum as most people could tell similar tales about their own kith and kin.

I have been fortunate enough to play with so many fantastic musicians through my career, and many I will mention when

1

needed to prove a point. But this will not be a name dropping, scandalous tale telling venture, you can read that sort of stuff elsewhere, and to be honest most of it is not my business, or relevant.

If I leave anyone out as I am sure to, I apologise unreservedly and will take the flak that will no doubt come my way.

I hope you enjoy your stroll through the archives of a jobbing musician, who has loved nearly every minute within the Blues fraternity, scoff and indeed laugh at my expense, feel free, I probably deserve it.

I have many people to thank, that have contributed to my career and life experiences, and I am sincerely grateful to each and every one of them.

FIFTIES

I was born in Longsight Manchester (England) June 21st 1950 the second son of Elsie and Frank Hume. My brother Malcolm arrived three years before me, which stood him in good stead when he later became a drummer as they always seem to come in first.

It was a happy childhood, like most kids growing up in an area that was rapidly running down, we didn't have a lot of money, but I can't ever remember feeling deprived.

The house where I spent my so called formative years was number 2 Norbury Street, a two up two down house, no garden and with an outside toilet. What we wouldn't have given for a soft Sunday supplement to soften the blow of freezing to death in the icy loo, and the fear of something jumping out on you from the winter sky in the back yard.

All the kids played football, and lots of other games. The most popular one I remember was called kick can, which usually ended up in tears after your parents had given you a clip round the ear for ruining your school shoes kicking the aforementioned can for all you were worth. We were like most kids slightly mischievous, but in a generally harmless way.

My interest in music started very early on in my life though I can't say it ran in the family. My Mother had many aborted attempts at piano lessons but was too busy helping to bring up everyone's children as well as her own, and my Father used to regale us with his musicianship or lack of it on the piano accordion, especially if we'd been naughty as a punishment.

As was normal for the time, our street was full of Aunties and Uncles, so it was hard to go too far off the rails. It was like being watched by a human CCTV spying out of every window, the lace curtains would twitch, and it was the equivalent of a telling off.

3

It was the time when a raised eyebrow from your mother could chill you to the bone. And wait until your dad gets home would cure the worst constipation.

I was really mad about the music of the time. Tommy Steele was my favourite. Ironically his version of Singing the Blues, was the first song I learned to play, and Connie Francis a very popular singer who even as a five-year-old I was already madly in love with having seen her on television.

Whilst on the subject of TV, I remember so well the day we had a set delivered to our house.

Before that never to be forgotten day, I used to call round to my friend's house under some false pretence and watch theirs. Ours was a Bakelite 9 inch Bush TV, we were so proud of it. I remember the first programme I saw on this wonderful invention was a Western or "Cowie" as we used to call them, 'The Cisco Kid' starring Duncan Renaldo in the title role and Leo Carillo as his happy go lucky sidekick Pancho. I though it was brilliant.

It is hard to believe how TV and for that matter cars have taken over since then. The TV stations used to close after the children's programmes finished so the family could all sit around the table for the ritual evening meal, which of course in the North of England we still call teatime, with dinner being lunch, we couldn't think of anything different for breakfast.

The BBC only broadcast for 39 hours a week until the ITV came along in 1955 in competition then they upped it to a massive 49.

The family meal rarely came to pass at our house as my Father was always working shifts at whatever job he was in at the time, either Engineering at British Steel or later on the buses, which I thought was really grand as we could get on his bus for free occasionally, a rider in the true sense of the word.

My Mum would be trying to catch the attention of my brother and I just long enough to throw some food down us before we disappeared back into the streets we had just come from, to

4

continue the game of Footy that had been temporarily halted by the Yell of Yoo Hoo from all the mothers. It was like a call to prayer.

I was always a big football fan, Manchester United has always been my team, although all my family were Manchester City fans. But I loved football in general, and in fact I went to see Man City bring the FA cup home on an open top bus after they beat Birmingham in 1956. It was the Final where the City keeper Bert Trautmann broke his neck and played on, long before the falling over and diving of today's players.

The FA Cup Final back then was a massive event, families used to congregate round the TV with the curtains drawn, and we would be glued to the box from about 11am until the Cup had been presented No video replays and catch ups back then, so it was the only chance we had to watch the Cup Finals from the past and of course the build up with the players on the coaches and so on. It was a memorable day for everyone.

The only other televised soccer we had was the England v Scotland match and all England Internationals that were played on a Wednesday afternoon.

My dad was a wonderful ally for me while I was feigning illness on an international day, and convincing my mother I was really ill, so we could watch it together on a Wednesday afternoon.

Of course, my mum always expected the bogeyman commonly known back then as the School Board who used to call round to check if kids were really ill and not playing truant. How times have changed.

I remember with dread Sundays, the first bit was OK, no school, and a nice lunch while listening to programmes on the Radio like the Billy Cotton Band Show, with the cry of Wakey Wakey. Al Read and Jimmy Clitheroe were also favourites of mine and massively popular, as was a comedic hero of mine Tony Hancock which was broadcast from 1954 to 1961, written by Ray

5

Galton and Alan Simpson who later went on to write the equally legendary Steptoe and Son. I have a signed book of scripts by them both, which is a much treasured possession.

Then the day took a turn for the worse. The smell of Cherry Blossom shoe polish still depresses me, which probably explains the state of my shoes.

The shoe cleaning was just a foretaste of what was to come, a trip to see my Gran who was a real disciplinarian, nice woman, but hardly known for her sense of humour, and a real matriarch. It had to be done for my dad's sake but it was one of the less pleasant parts of my childhood. Although my brother in fairness has very different memories.

The walk back home was a relief and I remember vividly watching Max Wall, the brilliant comedian, a true genius, on TV. Just when it couldn't get any better, it did, Swiss roll, or jam roly poly as we knew it and custard, it was the food of the Gods.

After an hour or so as the nights drew in, out came that instrument of torture, the Tin Bath, this was not good. It had been hung up in the yard all week, the rust was well in evidence, and it tended to infiltrate your more private nooks and crannies. It was all too obvious, that this was the night before school. Mothers had some quite torturous old wives' tales to inflict at the drop of an 'aitch. Mine was always looking down my ears, spitting on a handkerchief and washing my face with it.

The strangest of all, if anyone had a sore throat, she used to roll a piece of paper into a tube, put some sulphur in it, and blow it down the infected area. Not many germs would survive that, whether it did any good, I couldn't say, I couldn't speak.

There was also the threat of chilblains if you put your feet near the fire, especially after you had been out in the cold. I don't know how severe the temperature had to be to cause this reaction, but I never met anyone who had them. We used to put this weird waxy substance called Melrose on our toes to prevent whatever it was we were not going to suffer from anyway, it's no wonder we grew up silly. And as we were probably not getting enough vitamins that horrid mixture of cod liver oil & malt, was taken every morning yuk.

All in all, though I felt like I was having a pretty good time. I used to buy 78s records from a shop called Mazells on London Road, in Manchester and I didn't even care what records they were, I just loved the concept, and used to stare at the label designs for ages, as if they were a magical sign. I had a 78 of "Houndog" by Elvis recorded in 1956, and the ABC of Love by Frankie Lymon and the Teenagers from the same year, strange to think I was only 6 and already into quite adult music. Mind you I let myself down by buying Chesapeake Bay by Des O'Connor in 1957. Anyone can make a mistake.

The pop music of the day, which we all followed on Radio Luxembourg was our insight into the charts, the Top 20 Show, hosted by Australian Barry Aldis ran from 1958 to 1966, when Radio Caroline and other pirate Radio stations, more or less killed it off'.

It was really important to us growing up, we used to write the charts out in exercise books, charting the ups and downs, we were very, very obsessed. But then again we didn't have the gadgetry we now have to hear and see what we want when we want to.

So, there you have it, my childhood, pretty normal for the time, but I was very lucky to have such a solid family.

By the age of seven I was really interested in music from the radio shows mainly, pretty main stream kids' stuff, like the "Runaway train" Burl Ives and the like.

One evening my Mum came home with an Elvis Presley plastic guitar a friend had given her. It had what looked like an elaborate clamping device on the fret board, you supposedly pressed the appropriate chord name and it somehow would hold down the correct strings. Now this has many shortcomings, not least was that I didn't know what a chord was, other than the one holding my pyjamas up, and I didn't have a clue how to tune a guitar or what to, but it was a start.

I recall on one occasion when I was taken on a day trip to Southport, making a record in this pokey little kiosk accompanying myself (this time with a tin banjo). It is a great relief to all of us that the recording got lost, but ironically the title of the song was "Singing the Blues" a huge hit at the time for Guy Mitchell and the aforementioned Tommy Steele in 1956.

The actual disc which I was very excited to have made at the time, looked like the top of a Fray Bentos pie tin, and it had to be played with a wooden stylus of which you were only supplied with one. The most embarrassing moment of the whole event was at the end of the song shouting my name out, not through any egotistical fault of my own, it was what the automatic studio instructed me to do.

So flushed with the success of this recording, I remember playing this horrible tin Banjo for the duration of the coach journey home. The fellow passengers actually had a collection for me. I'm still not sure if it was through enjoyment, sympathy or just to shut me up. People were so kind in those days, now I guess it would take a good surgeon a few days to retrieve the offending banjo from my person.

Music always meant a lot to me, I used to get really excited when a church band marched past our street, I thought it was great, I even used to join in the Whit walks that were traditional back then, and Rose Queen parades too, in fact anything where there was music or some sort of event. One loud thud on a big bass drum and I was off to find the culprit, sorry, drummer.

We used to have money given to us by our families for wearing our best Whitsun clothes. There used to be a joke about a poor family buying their son a new cap and letting him look out of the window.

8

I put my money to very good use one year, 1961 to be exact, when I bought a 45rpm record of Adam Faiths "Easy Going Me". Fantastic, except we only had a wind up gramophone, so I used to wind it like a man possessed, then put my finger on the turntable to slow it down. It probably explains why I play everything too fast and all my records were scratched.

The volume control on the gramophone comprised of two wooden doors that covered the speaker, which you half or fully opened to suit, very ingenious.

They say that the ages of man come every 7 years, well mine certainly did. In 1957, whilst playing around in the garage at the back of my house with my lifelong friend Ian Stocks, I ran into a car in his Father's repair shop. Now I must state I actually did run into it. The car was stationary, but I managed to give my hip a really nasty wallop.

As all kids of that age, I didn't really worry about it too much but as the weeks became months, my leg was still hurting and was starting to give way under me more and more. So, as all good Mothers would do, I was dragged off to see the doctor, who on many subsequent visits came up with the same prognosis, it was just bad bruising.

Eventually my Mother's patience snapped and she forced the doctor to refer me to a specialist at Manchester's Gartside Street Hospital. After several X rays, the specialis,t and as far as I'm concerned, genius Doctor William Sayle-Creer, who sadly died in 1984, discovered that my hip bone had been gradually eroding in its own socket.

The first option for a partial cure at best would normally have been to encase the leg in plaster, But the specialist decided on another method as yet untried. For whatever reason I have a real hang up about plaster casts, an unusual phobia you may think, but I was open to any suggestions that didn't entail that.

As I was only seven years old the doctor believed that a plaster would restrict the growth of my leg. He decided what I thought impossible, I had to go to bed for eighteen months and under no circumstances, including going to the throne room was I to put my foot down. So, I was hopping everywhere, my left leg looked like an all-in wrestler and my right like a stick of celery, through lack of exercise.

As a child, one is very resilient and is always searching for any positives to any desperate situation. One of the real positives for me, if not for my parent's privacy, was that I had to have my bed moved downstairs into the living room as I couldn't possibly climb the stairs. So, pretending to be asleep I could occasionally risk one eye to see what adults watch on TV, so I quite enjoyed that. I remember getting into a mysterious detective programme called Mark Saber starring Donald Gray. I remember he had one arm, which sort of made it a bit more sinister, as he walked through the smog riddled London.

It was of little compensation for not being able to play football and the normal games kids played. My mates, who like most kids tend to have a low sympathy threshold soon stopped calling round so much.

That sounds really melancholy, but it didn't feel like that, I rarely had a black mood day, I'm sure I would now but somehow as a child you take things more stoically.

Christmas came and I had my usual batch of typical toys etc., but my father had decided, (and I never did find out why), to buy my brother and I a guitar each.

As mentioned before, we were not very well off so this was a real treat, or it would have been if the strings on the instrument could be made to touch the fret board.

This was an acoustic nightmare of epic proportions to play, it didn't even have the good grace to be a Spanish guitar as most acoustics were erroneously called. This was a masterpiece of Romanian engineered torture, but it looked great. It was sunburst which I really liked and the smell of the wood lives with me even now.

Missing school was another bonus, but only for a while as you miss you mates and what was much, much worse I started to get tons of homework to help me keep up.

In many ways I learned a lot that way without other children to distract me, but the urge to try and play this damn guitar was getting greater by the day. I find it hard to believe that Bluesmen on the delta like Robert Johnson could have had a worse instrument to play. But I was smitten with trying to tame this tortuous piece of wood, or to die trying. Literally my fingers would bleed sometimes but still I couldn't stop, it became a real obsession.

People still ask me today how often do I practise, I always tell them the same thing, I did more playing in my early years than most people do in a lifetime.

Eventually with a lot of trial and error, I managed to tune the guitar by ear to open tuning, and I used to bar the fret with my thumb, very unorthodox, although the late Richie Havens played that way for years and it did him no harm. It obviously was only in tune with itself, concert pitch was still a term I had yet to discover.

I got so much enjoyment from this fiendish instrument, and then one day the machine head cracked, and a pair of pliers became my next musical accessory to tune up with.

After the eighteen-month bed rest I went back to the hospital where things seemed to be going OK. The Consultant told me I could now walk on crutches for a further nine months.

Most people would still be a bit upset about the lack of freedom to run about, but I thought it was a vast improvement.

Of course, children can be cruel to each other and I got my fair share of abuse, the usual things and other less savoury things to do with people who are handicapped. I dislike that term even now.

After a while the teasing died down and I even learned to play a bit of football using my crutches like polo mallets. It gave me plenty of opportunity to even the score on some of my detractors by raking their shins instead of attempting to get the ball.

6th Feb 1958, will always be one of the most harrowing days in Manchester's history, when a plane crashed in Munich carrying the great Manchester United team. Eight of The "Busby Babes" as they were lovingly known perished. Rivalries between City and United were suspended and the city was united in grief.

For one of the finest ever young teams to die so tragically touched everyone, football fans or not.

As a seven year old, I remember so well my father coming home from work late, and telling me the news. The first thing I asked him was if Tommy Taylor was OK, He shook his head, I was devastated he was my favourite players at the time.

1950 My house in Longsight

The day it all started for me at the Talent Show in the 60s

SIXTIES

When it was summer, I used to spend quite a bit of time sat on the front doorstep still making a row with this same guitar By now there was a slight improvement, my cousin had a piano, so she used to tune my guitar to it. Unfortunately, someone had to take it by bus so by the time they got it back home, it was as out of tune at it was before.

Learning to play a guitar in the late 50's early 60's was not so easy as people find it today Very few people were playing them and certainly not anyone of your acquaintance. No YouTube to aid practice back then, so it was a slow process.

Everyone seemed to have a party piece the first one I remember was Shakin' All Over, by Johnny Kidd and The Pirates featuring the late great Mick Green, Then I suppose it would have been "House of the Rising Sun", Hilton Valentine of the Animals was responsible for this and even more recently I suppose it has to be 'Stairway To Heaven' or 'Smoke on the Water'

Who did I have at that time to look up to and be influenced by? Bert Weedon and Hank Marvin.

Bert was famous for songs such as Guitar Boogie. It did what it said in the title, like a boogie-woogie piano riff on a guitar, a simple idea that worked for him.

He was a national hero and he had the market more or less to himself, and was responsible for writing the most famous guitar tutor book *Play in a Day*.

Having seen Bert on a TV show, I wrote to the Studio and asked him for some help, like the poor guy had nothing better to do. He must have had thousands of letters from would be guitarists to get through. In fairness to him he did reply and sent me a chord sheet, which I was thrilled to receive, but ignorant of the content. It was like a foreign language, but methodically I learned the chords, frequently still out of tune, but I was starting to understand and hear relative pitch.

Bert later became an OBE and remained a hero to many of us until his death in April 2012.

I got to meet him a few times and he was very generous of spirit. considering I made a fool of myself (again) at a guitar convention, when awards were being handed around. It was the first sort of meeting of guitarist to be organized, not a good idea with alcohol freely available. It came to the presentation of the most popular Guitar Tutor, and again Bert's Play in a Day book won, I had been taken accidentally drunk at the bar and was speaking rather loudly.

When the Award was read out, I was heard to say (jokingly) "Anyone could play like Bert in a day", not noticing Bert was sat right behind me, Oops. To say the remark got a mixed reception is being kind, but I digress. Many years later we met up in a bar in Southport and he remembered what I said but was very magnanimous and thought it was quite funny too. So, we had made peace, he was a lovely man.

The Shadows featuring Hank Marvin with his use of the tremolo arm or Whammy Bar as it is known today introduced and inspired many up and coming guitar players, and along with the Ventures and Duane Eddy we were getting more access to what could be achieved on the guitar and various styles.

Still physically impaired leg wise, I ploughed on with my ultra-slow guitar self-teaching, unperturbed. I played until I wore my blisters to the bone. as Pete Brown once wrote in a lyric for Jack Bruce, or until my mother forced me to put the bugger down. I vividly recall sitting at the dining table with the guitar still on my knee, my good one that is, it must have driven the family out of their mind.

By this stage and understandably, my incapacity was starting to get me down a bit, so when my time on crutches of about nine months were up, I was optimistic that this time I would be passed fit.

Unfortunately, this was not to be, and the doctor prescribed a full leg calliper for another nine months, I was heartbroken, really for the first time. Although extremely uncomfortable, it gave me more freedom of movement, so much so I could go to a 'Special' school as it was known back then for all kinds of disabilities, to try and integrate kids back into the fold and pick up their education.

The school was the most amazing place, it was in East Didsbury Manchester called the Lancastrian. It had been set up by a tireless headmistress, Elizabeth Slinger, who now has a road named after her and rightly so.

The teachers did not molly coddle the kids and were quite stern, but it was probably essential for kids who have been out of touch with their peer groups in school to be treated with normality.

After the time was up on the calliper, I went back to the hospital to learn my fate. It was very low key I remember, and I was by now expecting the worst again. Dr Creer turned and twisted my leg every way but loose. My fear was he was going to damage the limb once again, but after much grimacing and dribbling into the pillow from me the words I wanted to here, though it doesn't sound so special now. The Doctor told me there is nothing more he can do, but as a 10-Year-old waiting for good news this sounded like a win on the lottery.

The feeling of walking out of that hospital on my own two feet so to speak, is one that will live with me always, and just to put the icing on the cake I had my first pair of new shoes for three and a bit years.

I felt like I had a lot of making up to do, and football was high on my recreational agenda, playing every free minute I had, it gave me a great sense of freedom it was like being reborn almost.

I was just a bit careful at first, but it soon passed, and I was soon as daft as ever throwing myself around with great relish.

So, I suppose the silver lining to underline my situation was the time I spent practising guitar while incapacitated. It didn't feel like that back then, but I suppose it did help me focus on something I was able to do.

Thankfully the music of the time was a wonderful mixture of styles from Elvis to Fats Domino, Ricky Nelson and of course the Shadows, every guitarist's idols of the age, so I was really hooked for the rest of my life to music.

Unfortunately, just as I had the euphoria of being able to walk properly my father's health was starting to deteriorate, slowly at first. He was diagnosed with lung cancer, and had to have a serious operation, I can remember the scar to this day, which went from the front of his chest under his arm and up his back. One thing really stuck in my mind, when he came home from the hospital was me throwing my arms around him not noticing the wound. It must have been excruciatingly painful but he acted like dads did in those days, and just shrugged it off.

But although we didn't know it at the time, the prognosis was not good.

Life has a wicked way of kicking you back down. In my case I had only just recovered from my injury, when one of the worst moments anyone has to endure is the loss of a parent, my Father died on April 15th 1961. I was not even eleven years old. I felt cheated as much as any other emotion. It seems strange after so many years have passed, how many wonderful memories he left me with, in such a short time.

My Mother somehow managed to cushion the blow and spent the rest of her life taking special care of my brother Malcolm and me. It must have been very hard for her with two sons, one just 13 and myself nearly 11 years old.

We had very little money and the benefit society was not working as well as it does today, but we were fortunate that my mother was the best manager of money I have ever known.

If she was the Chancellor of the Exchequer today, we would be very well off.

When my father died, it was not unexpected. He was a heavy smoker and unfortunately due to suffering a gas attack in the Second World War which had left him with no sense of smell, it had also obviously had a bad effect on his lungs. Regardless though it came as a shock, it's strange I remember so much about that day.

I had been watching the England v Scotland Football International at Wembley that afternoon, England won 9-3. I even remember the Scottish goalkeeper was called Frank Haffey.

There were several members of the family coming and going, so I knew something was happening. But nothing prepares you for the time when your poor mother, newly widowed, has to tell you your father has passed away. My brother immediately burst into tears, but I was just so stunned, I couldn't take it in.

The following day I remember was a particularly hot one, and I was sitting on the kerb on the main road on New Bank Street in Longsight alone. I must have looked a despairing sight, neighbours busily trying to keep your spirits up with, "You'll have to look after your Mum now, you are the men of the house". Although well-meant I just remember feeling burdened by the whole thing.

I seemed to cope OK until I went back to school the following Monday, and feeling a little tearful I excused myself and went to the toilets to compose myself. At that very moment a friend of mine appeared and said how sorry he was to hear about my Dad, and that was it, the tears were never ending for a couple of day. But somehow, as everybody is told when bereaved, time is indeed a great healer, and I think especially for children, who are already quite resilient as they have to be to make it through the whole growing up process.

At Christmas we got a record player thanks to my mum scrimping and saving. She never spent anything on herself. It was the most wonderful present I ever had, it was a Westminster from Curry's in Manchester, sort of fabric covered in turquoise. It was a magical, thing it meant so much when you have so little. It had a lot of use I can tell you.

By 1962 I had left the Lancastrian Special School, and was back in mainstream school, with plenty of catching up to do. However, I had a real thirst for knowledge having missed so much study time, and it was great to be back playing sports, and dreaming of one day being a Man United player, some chance.

Musically as time went on, I became more proficient through dedication, sheer hard work and pure, bloody mindedness. My mother was always supportive but not to the detriment of education and her belief that music was OK for a hobby, but not as a career, was indeed her mantra. Strangely enough, I never thought of it as a profession either.

The bug for being on stage started in 1963 when I was on holiday in Towyn in North Wales. We often went on caravanning holidays which I loved, particularly as I could play the juke boxes in the amusement arcades. It was very magical for a townie.
I still get a sense of excitement by the seaside even now, sad isn't it.

My Mum actually took me to see a summer season show featuring Heinz of the Tornados. It was a great night, and was feeding my enthusiasm to perform.

A few days later, on a day trip to Llandudno, we visited a veritable wonderland of that time called "Happy Valley". Long before the theme parks we know today, they had very light entertainment shows and Talent contests. The show was hosted by Alex Munro the father of actress Janet Munro.

Alex had managed and fronted the show there for years with a great deal of success. On the bill I remember was a group called The Statesmen, I even remember a song they played "Look Around". This is the life for me I thought, shows every day and permanently at the seaside.

My Mother, like many parents decided to enter me in the talent contest, which probably as a sympathy vote I won singing "Guess it doesn't Matter Anymore" by Buddy Holly which he released in 1959. I have only recently found out that it was written by Paul Anka when I decided to include it on the duo album with John Price 'Between the Lines' in 2013 as a reminder where it all started.

Alex Munroe was very impressed, or at least appeared to be and asked me to sing another song. The only one I could think of on the spur of the moment was the Welsh singer Ricky Valance's song from 1960 "Tell Laura I love Her". A great song, but a totally depressing theme about a guy called Tommy that gets killed in a stock car race, his hauntingly plaintiff final words calling her name.

Alex looked at the fairly elderly audience and made this great play about how someone so young could sing such an emotional song. The audience were close to tears, now whether this was of laughter or dejection I'm still not quite sure.

The prize for winning this competition was 10 shillings and a slot on the Lonnie Donegan show at the Gaiety Theatre in Rhyl, the same place I had seen Heinz a few days before, and there I was on the same stage. Who wouldn't be excited.

Lonnie was already a national treasure, and I was a massive fan, although most of the songs known to me were the quirkier ones like "My Old Man's a Dustman", and "Does your Chewing Gum lose its Flavour" etc. I soon discovered that behind these pop records Lonnie was indeed a great innovator, and his brand of skiffle is still as vibrant now as it was then.

The 10-shilling note or '10 bob' as we used to call it back then was great, but nothing compared to playing in this fantastic Theatre with Lonnie or Mr Donegan as he was to me, and ever since that day I have always experienced great excitement from just being in a theatre.

Lonnie also told me of a young folk singer I should listen to, so I did, the amazing Bob Dylan. His first album sounds as wonderful today as it did back then, when it was first released on March 19th 1962, a great mixture of Gospel Folk and Blues. This was actually the first album I ever bought, from a shop in Water Street in Rhyl. I was not too young to be impressed, although I found it slightly depressing, as a large percentage of the songs were about death, dying or graves.

Lonnie was always very supportive of me and indeed we worked many times together as guests with Van Morrison, who like myself had always been a huge fan of Lonnie. Getting back to theatres, I think I was probably born a couple of decades too late as I would have loved to have been in the Variety shows of the time, some of which I had been to see as a child. Acts like Norman Evans performing his 'over the garden wall' routine at the Ardwick Hippodrome, it was a character emulated by the great Les Dawson and Roy Barraclough in the Cissy and Ada sketches.

I knew after that night, that I wanted to perform on stage, but I was under no illusion how difficult it would be. As was usual in those days at school, some mates would get together and form a Skiffle band, and later in my case a 'Hollies' type harmony group.

Mum came through at Christmas again, this time with a tape recorder. It was magical being able to tape stuff off TV or Radio holding a microphone to the speaker, how times have changed.

It was useful to record bits of guitar also to check how it sounded.
It had its pitfalls too as my Mum overheard me swearing at my guitar on playback, tut tut.

My brother at this time was really getting into Blues music and used to tell me of some of the gigs he'd seen like Howling Wolf and Sonny Boy Williamson 2nd Rice Miller and they all seemed to me to be a bit strange and enigmatic and personally at this time I was still really into more mainstream pop music.

Being three years older than me, my brother was really into all kinds of music, and was playing drums in a band whose name escapes me, in fact it escapes him too.

After a few gigs, his band folded and with a couple of my mates and his we formed our first real group called **THE PROVINCES**. We were really pro, we even had business cards made with our names on each corner. How sad is that, and what a waste of money, as we soon changed the name to **THE SOUL SET**. This band featured Dave Brooks on bass who was a friend of my brothers and a joint acquaintance John McCormick on rhythm guitar and myself on lead.

Soul was the big music at this time especially in the North West where there were legendary venues such as Wigan Casino, the Twisted Wheel and the Oasis. In those early days any other sort of music was hard to sell, with the possible exception of folk and trad jazz, so even while we were not exactly playing Soul, the name Soul Set got us in the door.

We even obtained the services of a few agents. We were very proud of ourselves, probably wrongly, but we did quite a few gigs so we were doing it right in some ways. It was about this time when I bought my first harmonica, a harness, and a pickup, which was inside a rubber casing. It looked like a gas mask. I played it that very first night with no practice, at Browns Dance Club in Levenshulme. It must have shocked the Dancing hoards out of their Tamla Motown / Atlantic minds.

It turned out that I wasn't half bad on it for a novice, so it was another string or reed I should say to my bow.

On reflection, the Blues Brothers were not too far away from the truth. The guys on a night out on the pull wearing the new mod fashions of the day were not likely to be enamoured with a 12 bar blues, when they were expecting the best Atlantic and Motown Records had to offer.

23

We did make some concessions by playing a few Soul hits like Wilson Pickets "Midnight Hour" and "Shake" by Otis Redding. We salved our conscience however by playing them our way and buried in a set of R & B and the occasional hit like "Morning Dew" by Tim Rose to further put people off the scent.

Some gigs we got away with, but most we didn't, but it was a good apprenticeship for the times ahead. We played many of the Soul / Mod places in Manchester at the time such as Rowntree's Sound and Disco Takis and later the wind of change blew us into legendary gigs such as The Twisted Wheel and the Oasis. Both these gigs were coffee houses with no alcohol on sale, but as both venues used to hold all-nighters it became obvious that the pharmaceutical business was alive and well and living in clubbers.

These were quite heady times for musicians as respected bands of the day such as the Spencer Davis Group and John Mayall would both be on the same night for a very reasonable ticket price. The other good thing about these venues was they used to audition local bands and squeeze them on the bill, no money involved but the kudos was great and again it was a big help learning the business.

When I was about 15 years old playing at the Oasis, top of the bill was a really good band from Liverpool called the Koobas. I remember being really star struck just because they had made a record, you see I was naïve to a fault. They were nice guys and were a good band too. They sounded very polished unlike us, rough as hell.

Around 1963 / 64 and besides the music and football, I was really crazy about Speedway racing, which was a massive spectator sport at the time, and being a Belle Vue Aces fan also meant we could go into the world famous Amusement Park afterwards for free.

The fair was brilliant, but of course we were quite high spirited as teenagers, and some of us used to enjoy a go on the rifle range, while the stall holder was handing ammunition to someone else, we used to shoot up the prizes.

My own personal favourite occurred when a stray pellet hit an inflatable pig on the top shelf of the prize stall. Oh how we laughed as it scooted along the shelf knocking everything else off, and making a deflating scream on its way. Small things amuse small minds I know but I am laughing about it even now, I can still see and hear the whole scene.

Speedway is obviously very dangerous, but it was a shock beyond belief when the Aces maestro Peter Craven (the wizard of balance) died on Sept 24th 1963 after a freak accident at the Meadowbank Stadium in Edinburgh while taking evasive action to avoid hitting the fallen George Hunter.

All Belle Vue fans were devastated, and he was only 29. His death came only a year after he won the World Championship. Strangely enough years later I became friends with Ove Fundin, five-time World Champion, who is a big blues music fan and he told me that Peter was the hardest guy to beat on the circuit, and he should know. Although, he did add for any speedway fans amongst you, that Bjorn Knutson his Swedish country man was the hardest opponent if he got the gate as they say, or a good start to the lay person. They were great days, and they used to play the hits of the day in between races, so it had everything.

And on the way home a hotdog, to this day the smell of the methanol from the bikes and the fried onions from the hotdog stand should be bottled and used as a feel-good potion.

1964 was a time of the grimmest news in Manchester for many years with the Moors Murders in the headlines.

Longsight was a very close-knit community where everyone knew everyone else. Ian Brady was well known in the area, Although I never actually spoke to him, we used to see him quite a bit, and I remember pictures of Lesley Ann Downey everywhere after she went missing, and I knew Keith Bennett who was 2 years younger than me at the same school. Keith's body has tragically never been found.

It seemed every day was another bad news day, the drama seemed to last for ever. The relief that was written on everybody's face after Ian Brady and Myra Hindley were brought to justice, was tangible, a massive dark cloud was lifted. It never quite disappeared though.

To this day, people are unnerved crossing Saddleworth Moors, once a place of beauty, now a memory of evil.

It caused a real shift in the local mind set too. Neighbours who used to leave their doors open so anyone could call round for a chat, or borrow some tea and sugar were now very cautious. The innocence had gone, and people were very wary.

After all this drama, and in some ways in spite of it, the music scene was becoming very vibrant. It was also the year that really inspired me to play blues. A friend of my brother lent him an album with the caveat that he wouldn't like it as the guitar playing was a bit fast. The album was Five Live Yardbirds, and I loved it, so exciting and raw, of course speedy on the guitar was Eric Clapton. And on top of this new awakening the Rolling Stones first album had just been released. Musically they blew the door open to get a little bit more daring than the music we had been used to with the Beatles. Plus, the Stones upset parents even more which of course is always a plus being a teenager.

The Beatles came to the public attention in 1963 with the Please Please Me album which gave us a taste of what was to come. The Stones made sure they had the bad boy image working full steam, and it worked.

It polarised music lovers and it became a constant enquiry among friends Beatles or Stones?

I think it must be quite frustrating being a teenager in the 2000's when it's all been done before; it must be really hard to upset the parents that spent a generation upsetting their own parents with great success.

I absolutely loved that first Stones album in fact I liked the first 5 albums a lot, but I went even further with the how to shock the parent syndrome with my next favourite band The Pretty Things, I loved them.

They were raw full of attitude and swagger, I thought they were brilliant, and they had a manic Keith Moon like drummer in Viv Prince. Their debut single Rosalyn in 1965 was the first real new single I bought, and a great rendition of 'Big Boss Man' a Jimmy Reed tune on the flip side.

Phil May sadly passed away on 15th May 2020 he was a fantastic frontman and vocalist.

I had been messing about with a few local guys and trying to get a band together.

We got out first gig at Slade Lane Baptist Church in Levenshulme, Manchester. Only because they allowed us to rehearse there free of charge, that was the deal. We used to be there every Thursday night running through new chords as well as songs

We were just getting enough songs together for the show, when a row broke out, why or who with I can't remember. The upshot was the band of four split down the middle and tossed a coin to see who would do the gig. Unfortunately we won, as we only had a fortnight to find two more players.

We did manage it however, I remember very well being behind the curtain waiting to start. I could only hear the beat of my own pulse banging in my ears, but as soon as we started, I was fine, and we made a pretty good fist of it I think. Luckily it was such a long time ago I can't remember if we did or not.

We had to go to church the morning after the gig which was also part of the deal. And we were pretty satisfied with what we achieved, although I am not over sorry that the filming and subsequent uploading to YouTube of gigs that goes on today had not yet been invented, or we may have had to change our opinion.

It was a start, and I felt quietly confident I might be able to get a band together that would last for a while at least.

As 1965 arrived I had a newfound sense of freedom, just left school and working in an office, who were very supportive in my extra curriculum gigging, and occasional sicky or late arrival.

I remember being very jealous of Wayne Fontana at the time, as a girl I liked at school was always going on about him and how lovely he was. I met Wayne many times and it always reminded me.

My mate Ian Stocks had joined the band on bass. We had a forever changing personnel at this time, trying lots of people for suitability.

We did an unforgettable gig at Ardwick Youth Club, another suburb next to Longsight, and the following day some girls had found out where we lived and decided to just call round as if we knew who they were. It turned into a Carry On film, as their ardour was cooled by my mother pouring water on them from an upstairs window. Fans, especially girl fans were very fickle, you did not stay popular for long. In fact a great example was written on the local post office wall and as far as I know it is still there. It said 'Norman is Fab' as was the vernacular of the day, but a month or so later it was crossed out and said *'Norman is Shit '*. I think it must have been one of the girls that had been recently water boarded.

It was a very exciting time. We all thought we were going to be big stars, although unlike today being a celebrity was not the important thing, it was the music foremost and the girls of course. But we were hopeful we could have some success if we worked and practised hard, and this we did.

Rehearsals were always fun, more of a social gathering. We used to rehearse at the drummers' home, the house was a lot like the Bates Motel in Psycho, dark and imposing.

The drummer Len Piper was very good looking and a real babe magnet, and he was also absolutely crazy, but a lot of fun. I remember vividly when he came home late one night after a night with a couple of Watneys party fours as we used to get occasionally, and being slightly worse for wear, he decided to

28

sleep in a bed in the spare back room. He got in, passed out, and woke up next morning beside his dead Grandmother who had passed away during the night. He was a great lad and sadly he died quite young, a real character.

We were playing in various little bands at this time doing mainly youth clubs, which were very rough, but again it was a great way to learn not only about music and playing, but to toughen up a bit looking after yourself.

We were also doing a lot of church fete sort of gigs and our experiences were mounting up, and we were getting pretty good.

But the drummer met a girl who got pregnant and he took his responsibility very seriously and got a steady job to pay to keep them all.

I had become a massive Chuck Berry fan and was very excited to go and see him live on 10th January 1965 in Manchester at the Odeon, backed by Jimmy Powell and Five Dimensions who I really liked. Also on the bill, a band I came to know very well later the Graham Bond Organisation, with an amazing bass player. When Graham let him sing, wow. It was the genius Jack Bruce, it was a pivotal moment in my musical education.

Jack was a great friend and mentor for many years, I'm proud to say, we did some very special shows together, but more of Jack later. The Moody Blues and John Baldry were supposed to be on the bill too, but failed to make it due to transport problems, the announcer informed us. But Chuck volunteered to play longer to make up for it, and a huge roar went up, which was a bit unexpected. It was a night I will never forget. I later toured with Chuck in Europe, not the easiest man to get to know in the world, but who cares with his musical legacy. He really rocked, I was absolutely hooked on his R & B style.

The date was now 1966, and the world was a great place to be for a musician, and for England's football team. But being on holiday again in Wales, I missed the World Cup final and England beating the Germans 4- 2 at Wembley, typical. And

29

number one in the charts that day was "Out of Time" by Chris Farlowe, so it was a never to be forgotten song on a memorable day.

Blues music, had a real raw edge at this time, which appealed to me. I have always preferred music from the heart rather than the head. One thing Alexis Korner told me many years later was "Music should always have an effect, happy sad, whatever, it must mean something", and I have always played that way, and so I would give the same advice to any musician, make it count to someone. Try and make just a little difference to their lives, even if it's only for an hour or so.

We gigged just about every night. If we had a night off looming we wouldn't know what to do with it, so we would be on to one of the many agents that were booking acts like ours and get them to fill the date, regardless in many cases whether it was a suitable venue for us.

The fees were usually pretty poor, but you can't buy experience, and my God we were getting van loads of that.

As I have already mentioned we got to play some of the legendary venues when they were in their pomp, such as the Twisted Wheel, the Oasis, Takis, Rowntree's Sound etc. which was good going for some local lads.

The Twisted Wheel was probably '*THE* most legendary in Manchester and was open from 1963 to 1971. Founded by brothers Jack, Phillip and Ivor Abadi as a Blues and Soul live music club. The original location of the club was on Brazennose Street. It had no alcohol license, serving just soft drinks and snacks. There was another Twisted Wheel in Blackpool under the same ownership, but it was never as popular as the Manchester Wheel although I played it a few times.

It was rhythm and blues heaven, with Roger Eagle as DJ alongside the best live acts from the UK and USA. The club later moved to Whitworth Street.

Many of the records played at the 'Wheel' were rare even in America. In addition to the discs released by larger record companies, there was a huge number of releases by a wide variety of artists on a multiplicity of obscure, independent labels.

All-night sessions were held every Saturday, from 11:00 pm through. to Sunday at 7.30am

Each weekend at 2:00 am Soul artists performed live at the club. Junior Walker, Edwin Starr, Johnny Johnson and the Bandwagon, and Inez and Charlie Foxx were among the many musicians to squeeze onto the tiny stage. And I know first-hand how small that stage was, and how not to fall down any of the holes on it, something I failed to do more than once. Soul fans travelled from all over the UK for the all-nighters.

Following a visit to the Twisted Wheel in 1970, music journalist Dave Godin noted that the music played at the club, and in northern England in general, was different from the music played in London. His description 'Northern Soul' became the accepted term for this genre.

Everyone who was anyone played the Wheel. All the UK Blues greats starred or started there like Spencer Davis, John Mayall, Rod Stewart, Long John Baldry, even Cream played their very first gig there as a warm up. So, it was humbling to play on the stage that had featured so many greats.

In 2012 a film was made about the 'Wheel', and I was asked to contribute which I was thrilled to do. I was invited to the screening of the film and Ivor Abadi the originator and owner was there. I mentioned to him that as a kid I used to write to him every week to try and get a gig. He replied "I bet I always answered you too", I replied "yes, you always said NO". It was a really nostalgic night.

In 2013 the club finally closed for good, as the premises were to be demolished to build yet another hotel complex, very sad, The club was awarded a Blue plaque after much lobbying from fans, and now there is nowhere to hang it. We were honoured to be the last band to play the Wheel in 2012 when we did a very special gig with Chris Farlowe, who was one of the biggest mod icons back then, and so it was appropriate he finished things off.

31

So, at a rainy Manchester Sunday afternoon show, the streets of Manchester were in tears for the Twisted Wheel.

The Oasis was probably the next in legendary status, where I remember playing a few support gigs. It was always a good learning exercise to work with people like Lee Dorsey close up. Many huge stars of today got a break there even Tina Turner.

Other venues around at this time most of which we played were the Bier Keller, Jigsaw, Catacombs, Jungfrau, Mr. Smiths, The Bird Cage in Ashton, Bolton Palais, Cheetham Hill Ice Rink, (what a strange place that was by the way, sweating through the exertion of playing, and the next minute freezing when somebody skated past you and caused a right draft,) Quaintways in Chester, The Oaks in Chorlton, Droylsden Top Ten, The Bluebell, The Bamboo in Hazel Grove, and many more.

Quite often a band would promote their own gigs, where the landlord would let the band or promoter have the room free. The band would keep the door takings and the pub would take all the bar sales. This worked out pretty well for everyone, and bands such as ours started to create an interest and a bit of a following. This in turn led to the odd TV slot and a bit of Radio.

At this time we would play any kind of gig that would book us, and although you hear a lot of terrible stories relating to the Working Men's Clubs, many of them true I might add, I used to really enjoy playing them. Not because of our set, but I could see the other performers comedians etc. and it took me back to the old Variety kind of shows again, and you got a game of bingo and pie and peas for your trouble. Rock & Roll or what.

It was interesting to find that a 'wannabe' Frank Sinatra style crooner, was more rock and roll off stage than we were on it. We used to often give some of the acts a lift in our van, and their behaviour was sometimes appalling, and we were not easily shocked.

The MC's and comperes were brilliant, some of their comments were great. Post Hendrix I played the guitar with my teeth (for real) not like Jimi hammering on the strings. Many a

32

time there was blood on my scratch plate. The compere said and I quote "That was amazing ladies and gentlemen, he really played that with his nose". I suppose it's a new slant on playing by ear.

Ian Stocks reminded of the time at a working men's club when they held an emergency meeting to decide whether our respective girlfriends could come in as their skirts were on the short side, I think the judgement of Solomon decreed, it was OK as long as they kept their coats on, brilliant.

1966 was also the year that turned many people of my age into Blues mad fools for ever with the release of John Mayall's Bluesbreakers with Eric Clapton. In my opinion Eric has never played better than this. Iit was raw and emotionally to the point, from first song to last this album oozed class and raw power. Even bands born decades later still believe it was a defining moment in UK Blues, and I am certainly in agreement.

In 1967 I had to go in hospital for a nose op, as the bone was growing sideways and it would eventually have been impossible to breathe through, so off to the ENT in Manchester. There was no real problem with the surgery until I opened my big mouth and asked the surgeon exactly what he had done. He started to tell me in graphic detail how he broke it with a little mallet, drilled a couple of holes etc. I was really sorry I asked, take my advice, never try to find details out, better not knowing. One ironic moment in this escapade was on the hospital trolley after some sedation, on the way for the op what came on the Radio? "Oh Pretty Woman" from the new John Mayall album Crusade, So as soon as I got out of hospital I was down the record shop post haste for my copy. It was another great album with Mick Taylor on guitar this time

Around this time, we decided to change the name of the band, as Rhythm & Blues bands such as the Stones, Yardbirds, Pretty Things etc. caught the masses imagination and proved to us there was a life playing the music we loved so much. So, after a bit of a disappointing gig at a Soul club, we decided to come clean and instead of playing a safe mix of soul & blues, we were from this moment going to play what we wanted to, raw Rhythm & Blues, the Rubicon had been crossed.

We struggled for weeks to find a suitable name for the band and we finally decided on **MORNING AFTER** which was a song we found on an album by the Mindbenders.

The personnel had changed little since the Soul Set with the exception of the aforementioned Ian Stocks on bass. We had always been close. We used to go on holiday with each other's families when we were young, and Ian's Dad Terry, used to often drive us to gigs a lovely man very kind, he lived in the next street to me.

Ian and myself both learned to play guitar about the same time and in fact we even made the same positional chord shape errors. We used to always be in each other's houses learning new chords and songs.

Every Friday night Ian would come to my house or vice versa to watch the now legendary television show Ready Steady Go and have supper while watching it. From the moment 5-4-3-2-1 by Manfred Mann heralded the show, the programme was exciting and I might add that in my humble opinion has never been bettered for pure live music and atmosphere.

It only ran from 1963 to 1966 but these were ground breaking times where the Stones, Beatles, Kinks, Animals etc. just used to turn up for an impromptu session.

It was hosted by Keith Fordyce and Cathy McGowan, and had a massive effect on the music scene, making albums important as well as singles. If only a show like that could be replicated today, but most record companies and managers don't want to risk a poor performance at close quarters. RSG certainly opened up the market for good live bands as against the manufactured pap every generation has to suffer.

This is a short list of artistes that performed on the show

The Who, The Beatles, The Hollies, The Zombies, Dusty Springfield, The Supremes, The Temptations, The Walker Brothers, The Kinks, Gerry and the Pacemakers, The Rolling Stones, Donovan (discovered on RSG) The Fortunes, Helen Shapiro, P.J.Proby, Otis Redding, Dave Clarke 5, Bobby Vee, The Animals, Cilla Black, The Searchers, Georgie Fame, Billy Fury, Marvin Gaye, Gene Pitney, The Beach Boys, Sandie Shaw, Burt Bacharach, Jerry Lee Lewis, The Small Faces, James Brown, Chris Farlowe, Jimi Hendrix also made his TV debut with "Hey Joe" and many more.

So, we had all been watching the same bands and had a good idea what we wanted to do. We then added John McCormick on rhythm guitar, who again was a close friend and we all lived within 10 minutes walking distance which was of course great for getting a quick getaway, to a gig when someone had cancelled.

We started gigging pretty heavily right away. The time was right for a blues band thankfully, there were a lot of us budding blues acts, but plenty of gigs to go round.

Agents soon became interested in Blues bands or R&B as it was called then, before today's confusion as what R & B music really is.

We were doing OK, all mates having a good time doing what came naturally, then we saw an advert to audition for a new TV show called First Timers at Granada Studios

The show was produced by Johnny Hamp who later went on to be head of light entertainment and produced programmes for Granada such as The Comedians. He was a genuinely nice bloke and a real enthusiast.

We had to audition in the TV studio which was really nerve racking. You have to remember that this was the time when failure was not the viewing spectacle that we now have with Pop Idol, X Factor and all that celebrity cra., Oh no, you failed with dignity in those days, and fail we did, but being tenacious I found Johnny's address and told him I thought he had made a mistake, and lo and behold he gave us a second chance to fail, and we did not let him down, we failed.

I remember that Amen Corner went on to win the show. There were some really great bands around at that time vying for positions. Another band that came from that show were The John Evan band some of whom later became Jethro Tull.

It was in 1968 that Ian had to leave through work commitments. He had started a haulage Company that was now taking too much of his time to be touring. He did however go on to be become one of the finest country bass players around and he didn't have to travel so much.

One incident that will live with us all for ever was a gig we played at the Beachcomber in Liverpool where Ian received a massive electric shock when the machine heads on his Fender Precision caught on the microphone stand. He was thrown to the floor, his hands burning on the strings, as is always the case your muscles freeze and make it impossible to let go. As he was blown backward, he hit the cymbal which my brother tried to grab, and he too was blown backwards as the current surged through it. The stage was a scene of carnage. I found the plug socket and just kicked the plug out; I was half expecting me to get a shock too. It was a very traumatic experience.

We advertised in the Manchester Evening News for a bass player, and a guy called Paul Pearson from Wythenshaw applied, and we immediately loved him and his playing. He was nicknamed Barney due to his resemblance to Barney Rubble from the Flintstones and he was never known as anything else. He was already in a band but was looking for something different, and he fitted in perfectly.

TV or not we were really starting to make a name for ourselves albeit locally. We decided with our Commer van to go to the capital and play a few auditions for agents, record executives and the like. We came back with nothing concrete but with a positive attitude, which unfortunately did not stretch as far as our van which we had to abandon on the way home somewhere near Northampton.

Liverpool was a hot bed of venues, and we used to play at most of them, often for the whole weekend. Of course, we could not afford hotels and the like so we used to travel down on Fridays as soon as we had all finished our various day jobs, most of which were just too boring to talk about, and play a late night club. When the gig was over about 2am we used to drag our feet as much as possible stripping the equipment down and loading our now third Commer van.

We then went to the Pier Head and whiled away our time in various all night cafés, my own particular poison at this time was a mug of Horlicks to warm me up. The band used to joke about me being asleep when it was my turn to pay.

We then found the nearest cinema to fall asleep in until it was time to go to the next gig. We were probably filthy, smelly, and certainly worse for wear. I reckon I must have slept through more films than anyone alive, even today when I visit a cinema, which is very rare admittedly, I can feel my eyelids drooping It's a bit like Pavlov's dogs.

We were making progress, but still lacking the recording contract that may change things quickly. We did the usual things, sending tapes to various A & R men who very rarely listened. In fact just for fun on occasions we would tie a bit of cotton round the spools, and nine times out of ten the cotton was still intact when we got the tape returned and the stereotypical letter which went something like 'Thank you very much for your interest in our label, however although we enjoyed it immensely, it is not quite what we are looking for at present'. It's amazing how you can send blues songs to a blues label and be told it's not what they are looking for.

60's Morning After 60's
L to R Ian Stocks, Malcolm Hume, John McCormick and me in front

1969 Morning After
L to R Paul (Barney) Pearson, myself, John McCormick and Malcolm Hume

SEVENTIES

As well as musicians, there was a great subculture of friends, that doubled up as roadies, so many characters, just your mates, who wanted to come with the band for a laugh, and generally pick girls up before the band got to them. We had some real treasures, I will keep the names to myself to protect their identities, as they may now be in respected employment.

On one occasion we actually decided to interview a driver, who seemed really nice, and he was into the music and the fun of being on the road. We pulled up at an all night Café on the Yorkshire Moors for a brew, it was winter, and freezing. As we turned the engine off, a police car approached, the officer was obviously of the old school, stiff upper lip etc. "Do you know you don't have any road tax". We all looked in disbelief. The driver said "so what, I don't need any, I'm not on the road". Not the best way to speak to Mr Plod I thought, "Well, lad how did you get here in the first place?" Oops, this was not going well, we all looked at the ground for mercy. Again the driver came back with a cocky answer "I just wished and wished". We were trying not to laugh, but it was a great answer. "OK son, where's your license" and the reply came back with a smile, "I'm still wishing for that". With that aside he was hauled off by the police, though they did give us permission to take the van home and take all our paperwork to the police station later that week.

You would have thought that having interviewed this guy we would have had enough oil in our can to actually ask him if he had a license.

We seemed to attract some real pranksters as mates come roadies, one of my favourites was a good friend of Paul 'Barney' Pearson. The roadie of whom I speak Danny Farrell was a fantastic driver could turn vans round in cul- de- sacs by going half way up a wall at the end and flipping it round, brilliant, but very scary.

But his absolute finest moments were spent, showing off by climbing into a tumble dryer and getting someone to turn on the machine as he rocked to and fro with his face pressed against the port hole window. How he lived through this madness is anyone's guess, but he would do it at the drop of a coin in the slot, a true nut case but a lot of fun.

We had a crazy Irish guy too, who was right up there with the best of them. He found an Alice band with light bulbs on it, in the dressing room at a school gig. To much consternation of the crowd and whist having an afro hairstyle, popular at the time, he combed it over the head band, and with a battery in his top pocket occasionally touched the wires and lo and behold his hair lit up. What a burke!

His timing however was perfect, he waited until he saw a nice looking girl looking then "Flash" and he would stop and watch her try to explain to her mates what she's seen. Of course he didn't do it again until she was the only one watching, so everyone thought she was crazy.

He also had a liking for a megaphone he had found somewhere, and in the dead of night many cries of obscenities could be heard from this giant among roadies. He was fearless too. He once got us to drop him off, on the Yorkshire Moors, and we stopped at a café come garage a little further on. We had no idea what he was up to, but cars were screeching to a halt at the café, and people were looking very shaken. It transpires he had covered his head with a blanket like a monk and was standing in front of vehicles and then jumping down the side of the road, a true barm pot. The people that had been "Ghouled" as he called it, were telling us all about their trauma.

Not only "roadies" were things legends were made of, so was the lack of suitable accommodation on the road.

One weekend in the Northeast that has left an indelible impression on my memory was when we had 4 gigs over one weekend.

The first was at a gig in Newcastle called the Nova Castrian. We drove past the venue looking for the get in door, and I watched open mouthed as one coal miner took the helmet off the guy he was talking to and whacked him a hefty blow with his own helmet. God I thought what have we let ourselves in for, but it was fine, rowdy but otherwise OK.

Off we go to Sunderland to our 'digs' as would be hotels were aptly known back then, knackered after the drive and the show, to be greeted by Florie, who was stood there in her airtex vest and pants with a fag in her mouth. She was a diamond and she knew exactly where we were all playing and what time we had to be there. Her organisational sense stopped there. She said to us "E' you must be starving lads I'll make ya some tea". Some hope a round of bread and butter, and for a washing facility a galvanised bowl of luke warm water for us all.

The toilet situation was no better, it was outside and we were four floors up, so Flo's husband gave us a bucket in case. Of course, only yours truly needed to go in the night, and managed to wake up everyone with the clatter like a fountain on a corrugated tin roof.

The following morning was very showbiz, lots of Stage mags etc. mainly covered in marmalade, jam and other stuff I don't want to contemplate on. There I spied a stripper, chatting to her, probably bullshitting like we do, when Mr. Florie walked in with the bucket walked straight up to me and told me to empty it in the loo, him 1 my image 0. The rest of the band were merciless in making fun of course, which was to be expected.

But worse was yet to come, our hostess brought in a full English something, I couldn't call it breakfast, it looked like a bad case of road kill. However game and hungry as I was, I thought the sausage looked like the best bit, it wasn't. Not wanting to upset Flo I waited for her to leave the room, then lifted the window overlooking the front garden, and scraped the whole lot onto the lawn. I could not believe my eyes;
the garden was full of rotting food from everyone who stayed there doing the same thing.

The following day's gig was at Durham University, and we went down an absolute storm, one of the best gigs we had ever played. When we returned to the 'digs' Flo told us tomorrow is an early gig first backing a stripper and doing half an hour on our own.

What an eye opener that was on every level, we backed two exotic dancers as the ladies prefer to be known. One was gorgeous, so we played a very slow sensual bit of blues for her, took about 15 mins, then another came on, not such a looker, and I was all for playing the "Sabre Dance" and the "Flight of the Bumble Bee" to get it over and done with, but we stuck it out, so to speak.

That night's gig was at Hebben Memorial Club, sort of Working Men's Club. We got on stage, played pretty well, and we thought all was OK when the compere said, how do you think it's going lads? We replied so-so, he said, "afraid not guys here's your money, have an early night and give us all a break, I'm unbooking you". It sounds so funny now, but at the time, we were really puzzled, so it was a mixed bag.

Thankfully I seem to have cracked the North east now, but I learned it the hard way. Especially after several slurps of Exhibition beer.

A John Mayall concert in Manchester was always a really special event and he was selling out everywhere, without having to sell out himself. I have met him many times and he is a great guy. We of course treasure John as he was from our region in fact only 10 minutes from where I live, a hard act to follow.

Over the next few years we were gigging all over the country with a fair amount of success and along the way met and played with various luminaries of the Blues world like Victor Brox, Graham Bond and Alexis Korner.

It was a great time to be in a band, there was a very fraternal atmosphere between the groups, and everyone was genuinely pleased to see the other getting on.

We used to meet up with a lot of our contemporaries in Manchester in the early hours, in the Wimpey Bars coming back from late night venues, and we had a great time chewing the fat literally with the other musicians.

On many occasions the trips home from gigs were very amusing. It was a cross between the Keystone Cops and Silverstone, as painted vans took turns in overtaking and shouting at each other in a friendly way of course, and enquiring where you had been playing, there was a lot of banter all good fun.

On one occasion on our way back from St Helens, a van overtook us jeering and shouting. So we returned the gestures as was expected in response and overtook them, then again they came, really screaming, so we decided we better sort it out. We overtook and pulled up with a scream of brakes. They pulled up some distance behind, "what's the problem" we shouted, and the response was "your vans on fire", and it was too, how we didn't blow ourselves up is anyone's guess.

Of course, vehicles in those days had to be bought cheap and we did work them to death. I used to like the red J4 post office van we had for years, as the engine was in between the 2 front seats, and as I was the smallest, I was in the middle, and very warm with an overheating engine

We progressed to the Commer next, this was a proper van, windows and everything, we bought it from the Blind Society. I never quite understood why it had windows at the time. Anyway, we thought we were really big time now.
We finally ended up with a fairly new long wheel base transit, which unfortunately seized up on its maiden voyage, so now we were really in trouble.

It was a very worrying situation loads of gigs, no van, still paying for the thing even though it was kaput, I remember it was a bleak time indeed. We were sat stranded in a café. We really thought this was the end, until a friend of ours Kevin Smith offered to buy a van and drive us and we would pay him per gig. It really did save us from having to come off the road. Don't know what we would have done without Saint Kevin.

The houses in Longsight where I was still living were now in line for demolition. We feared the worst, as the alternative accommodation was a high rise horror that was nicknamed Fort Ardwick. It was a place nobody wanted to go to, it was sad to see so many extended families and good friends being split up and sent to various overspill estates. It caused a lot of upset and loneliness.

It was by absolute good luck that we managed to get a rented house in a nice part of Burnage via the Co-operative Housing Association, really nice garden front and back, inside toilet, bathroom, what luxury. Every day was like living in a hotel to us.

It was well earned reward for my mum too. We bought her a washing machine to celebrate, it was the equivalent of the Crown jewels to her.

The locals were great too, we used to frequent the Victoria Inn on Burnage Lane and had lots of fun nights, we made many good friends there. It's a shame we didn't get there sooner.

Eventually in 1971 we took the bull by the horns and recorded an album called **"Blue Blood"** which we paid for ourselves. It turned out to be a good move as we sold loads at gigs and of course made the profit.

This was really the beginning for my song writing, All the songs on this album were written by myself alone or with another member. By this time the line-up had changed yet again, Malcolm was still on drums, Mike Corrigan on keyboards and Steve Tanner on bass.

The album was a bit of a mixture, but we learned a lot and quickly. It has recently been released 50 years later by someone unbeknownst to me all over Europe and people are regarding it as a wonderful example of Underground Blues. I think raw and badly recorded is nearer the mark, but if they like it good on them.

We played all over the country with this line up in the late 60's and early 70's, and played every single night for 2 years, now that is an apprenticeship. Gradually we got into promoting gigs too. One example was the Bier Keller in Manchester, which we used to run on a weekly basis, and we would play and have guests bands on, it cost us a fortune, and we had to do more gigs ourselves to pay for it. But we enjoyed the experience.

We invited many people to play there, it was a great atmosphere. I remember Bill Nelson of Be Bop Deluxe fame playing with a band called Shiva, and also a guy who was to have quite an unexpected effect on my career Victor Brox.

Victor had been running his own band the Blues Train for many years in the 60's, and was well respected as a great singer, keyboardist, pocket cornet and violin player and quite a character

I had seen him play a few times and loved his voice. He had been vocalist, keys player with the Aynsley Dunbar Retaliation throughout their existence from1968. He really came to people's attention, when people like Janis Joplin and Jimi Hendrix claimed he was their favourite singer.
He went on to play Caiaphas the high priest on the original Jesus Christ Superstar album in 1970.

He returned to Manchester shortly afterwards and reformed the Blues Train Many people owe Victor a lot, myself included for letting wet behind the ears muso's get up and have a play.

We continued to promote gigs at the Bier Keller and the Shoulder of Mutton in Todmorden, but we were having to work so hard to sustain the venues we eventually had to admit defeat. But it was by no means a failure, we had found some great bands and given them venues with open minds and good atmospheres to hone their craft.

Morning After as a unit was getting a bit tired, musically, not of each other. I even decided I was going to pack it in altogether as I was so knackered, or at least have a long rest. My brother decided he was going to take a break and hitch around Europe with his mate, so it seemed a good time for us all to take a breather.

I was so determined to do something else I even advertised in the Manchester Evening Newspaper to sell some of my gear. I got a call from a band from Nottingham called Woody Kern I think, and when they came to see me, they persuaded me not to sell, I was so touched I gave it some more time.

Within a fortnight I was back playing with renewed vigour, it was a very strange time, and it was the last time I ever even contemplated stopping playing.

My Mother had been diagnosed with Cancer and we had to look after her for a couple of years on and off. She finally succumbed to the illness in the April of 1971.
She was a wonderful woman and certainly instrumental in my career, never pushy but always supportive, always encouraged us to get on with our own lives even when she was so ill herself.

She was also a friend to the musicians that would drop in when they felt like it, and they could be sure of some nourishment. It was a very hard time.

It also changed the whole dynamic of the family unit obviously, as my brother had a girl friend who used to stay over. I had one that would stay over, and so it was a bit fraught at times.

I decided I wanted a place of my own and moved to a really nice flat in Heaton Moor, a nice area of Stockport that I always liked. It was very strange after the death of my Mum, the house never seemed like a home to me anymore, so the leaving was like a weight lifted off me and a new start, in every way.

It soon became noticeable how much I had things done for me when I had to start cooking my own meals. I once made a risotto and put the rice in the frying pan as I had seen people do however,

I hadn't boiled it first and I was being shot at by scorching hot rice pellets.

I enjoyed living on my own for a while, it was a good time to reflect and also plan or try to see what to do next. Music as anyone will agree is very hit and miss, and quite unpredictable, so a lot of luck as much as judgement is essential.

In 1973 I drifted or was conscripted into the **Victor Brox Blues Train**, and the Morning After venture sadly started to play second fiddle for me as the work with Victor was coming in thick and fast

I played and recorded with Victor for years, until about 1977. It was during this spell that we were asked to do a music spot on Granada Reports, the regional news programme. It was just a three-piece Victor, Annette Reis (Victors wife) and myself. We were promoting Victors "Rollin' Back" album released in 1974 on Sonet.

I was supposed to be playing a gig with someone else that day, but I really fancied doing this TV slot. So, I dressed in this horrible orange paisley shirt, and wearing my hair long at the time, I let it fall over my face with my head down as much as possible to hide my identity. It didn't work, later that night a drunk coming out of a pub I was entering said, 'I saw you on TV tonight' so that was it, cover blown, luckily there were no repercussions.

A couple of days prior to this, knowing that Victor Brox wasn't his real name, he explained how he chose it. Victor was his middle name, and near Bonfire Night he saw an advert for Brocks Fireworks, and decided to re spell it Brox, as the letters would be bigger on a poster.

Joining in with this theme I suggested I should change mine, and he replied in his most disgusted tone. 'Norman the only people to conquer Britain and Hume a great British name, you could be a direct descendant of the Beaker Folk.'

So, wind back to the TV spot, Brian Trueman the presenter asked Victor the name of everyone, and Victor just said Norman Beaker, and that was it.

Over the next few days and because of this TV show I was asked to do loads of work, "
'Can I speak to Norman Beaker', 'Is Norman Beaker there' and so on, and that was it, and it has been that way ever since.

During my time with Victor, many musicians came and went, some I still see and play gigs with today, some joined my band later. Victor and myself played in many different formats from duos, trios, big bands it encompassed everything. We were playing a lot of residencies too. Every Sunday we used to play at the Surrey Arms in Glossop, which at the time was a very in place, even the Maharishi had moved into the area. It was a great time, and many people I meet to this day all over the world remember these sessions.

On occasions the late legendary pop / artist David Vaughn used to paint murals on the walls while we played, a sort of multi media event ahead of its time. For the uninitiated Dave was the guy who painted John Lennon's Rolls Royce, in psychedelic designs. He unfortunately died in 2003, he was also the father of actress Sadie Frost.
He painted a great wall sized mural of the band, which was found under redecorated wallpaper many years later.

It was at this time I met my first wife Carol, she was at college at the time. We hit it off right away, although she never forgave me for saying to one of her friends "Who is the old bag in the black shawl" oops.

Gigs came thick and fast with Victor. He was always picking up residencies, and we had one we did as a duo in Ashton-under-Lyne three times a week called the Old Dog, and would of course do the Surrey Arms on a Sunday with the band.

48

I was persuaded by Carol to go with her to see Genesis at the Palace Theatre. This I was not keen to do, but queued up most of the night for tickets anyway.

I was so glad I did. It was the best Concert I had ever seen from all aspects, the theatricals which I loved of course, and the music too, it was the Lamb Lies Down on Broadway tour.

Would you believe it, I was given two free tickets for the night after, but I was happy to go again believe me it was brilliant. I recently met up with Steve Hacket and we had a good reminisce of the shows.

By 1976, I had become pretty synonymous with Victor, and we made quite a good double act in the band, a bit of good humoured banter was never far away. It also led to me working with a lot of US blues artistes that were being booked by Jim Simpson at Big Bear in Birmingham, and Chris Lee who besides writing for the Manchester Evening News had started booking some gigs at the Birch Hall Hotel in Lees.

Victor's band were the sort of house band, we played with Eddie Guitar Burns and the wonderful Jimmy Witherspoon, which was a great thrill. He was always one of my idols, and he gave me loads of solos which was unusual as he was more brass oriented, so it was a bit like winning the lottery for me, I had a great time. We also worked with Gene "Mighty Flea" Connors, the man who took trombone playing to another level with his unique triple tonguing technique and can be seen in the Clint Eastwood "Play Misty for me" with Johnny Otis.

On the day of the gig, we arrived a bit late, and with about half an hour before show time, Victor asked Gene if we should have a quick run through, he blankly said no. "We have a day's rehearsal or none." So, none it was, but he was a great leader and it was a fantastic night.

This was the time of the legendary Granada TV show 'So It Goes', the programme hosted by Tony Wilson, a long-time friend of mine and Clive James. I had been on my holidays in Italy and the day I got back I got this emergency call from Victor to get down to the studio. All I had with me is what I was stood up in,

49

a pair of red clogs, sky blue jeans and an old T-shirt. It caused much hilarity to see the wardrobe woman trying to iron my gear while I was in various stages of undress, it was beyond image by then.

We performed with Eddy "Guitar" Burns, I never quite understood why he was called that as he played mainly harmonica.

We made a second performance on the show this time with the great harmonica player Snooky Pryor, who was fantastic. As is the way of most Blues musicians, songs have a pretty indeterminate length, you stop when you have said all you want to say and not before, and Snooky did exactly that, it went on and on. The producer asked if he could cut it down to 3 ½ minutes "Yeah no problem". So, he said "Miss the outro, miss a verse and one less solo". We obeyed, and guess what, dead on 3½ minutes, what a professional performer.

Also on that show were Kate & Anna McGarrigle, I watched dumbstruck as they were rehearsing their set. Their voices were truly beautiful, and I had a rare moment of being really tearful listening to them. I subsequently met them a few times and told them this story.

By the time we went on to do our song, my eyes were blood red from blubbering over Kate & Anna. I still have to be careful where and when I play their records for fear of making a fool of myself (again). Kate died in 2010, and her sister sent me a lovely message which I cherish to this day.

1977 turned out to be quite a year professionally and personally. I married my first wife Carol, and also decided it was time to move on from Victor. I was writing a lot of songs and felt it was the only way to get them played.

When I look back it looks a bit like an act of treachery, I took with me, (though I have to say willingly" the drummer Tim Franks and the bass player Dave Lunt from his band and another old friend on guitar John Dickinson who sadly passed away in

2013. I had by this time worked with a lot of quite well known players such as Jon Lord, Graham Bond and Tony Ashton who all remained great friends until their premature demise.

Some of my songs were quite jazz influenced and I had been painted into a corner a bit playing straight ahead 12 bar Chicago blues, so I decided to make a stand, and after listening to a 'Return to Forever' album **NO MYSTERY**. I decided to use this title for the name of the band.

The band performed its first gig on March 3rd, and it was really good, it was everything we were all looking for musically, original slant on Blues and Jazz. Then after only a few months of gigging with this line up, John Stedman of JSP Records phoned me and asked if we would like to perform on the legendary UK television show "The Old Grey Whistle Test" with Louisiana Red. Well you don't say no to either.

On the day of the Whistle Test, on November 1st which was broadcast live, it was really exciting, and a really good break for us. Bob Harris was the host, and was well known for his unflappability, well not with Louisiana Red and his wife Odetta on the studio floor.

First of all, Odetta was strutting around the floor in a big fur coat taking no notice of where the cameras were, and Red, well he was just always very unpredictable.

Bob briefed us all, that there would be a clip of Graham Parker, he would then talk at the end, then introduce us.

So, there is Bob very cool in his swivel chair, the Graham Parker film finishes. But before Bob can announce us a slide in the Elmore James style blares out, Bob whizzed round on his chair and garbled at high speed "Ladies and gentlemen, Louisiana Red and No Mystery" over this rocking Blues band. I have never seen Bob move so quick.

It was 30 years before I ever saw our performance, when it was used as a promo for a Festival.

51

So, within months we were now being seen as a Blues band again, and to be honest at that time we were pretty much on our own as far as Blues bands went.

The jazzy name did not stop me from following what was obviously going to be my calling, playing the Blues, and that's what I have done ever since and never again tried to confuse matters.

I have always tried to write songs that are lyrically in tune with today's events, as I see them. Having never worked on cotton plantations or share cropping etc. I can't write about such things with any conviction.

I just do what all the blues singers from the past did and write about my own environment and life experiences.

We were working so hard, playing so many gigs to many people who as yet were not so conversant with Blues music unlike today. So, we really did pay our dues with that band, but thoroughly enjoyed the experience too.

One of the highlights of this time musically, had to be a concert with the legendary pianist James Booker from New Orleans, a true great. He was brought over again by John Stedman, we became the house band for many of the touring US Bluesmen through this connection.

Booker was a heroin addict, (recovering) when he came over and a couple of times had to leave the stage to vomit, but his playing was as immaculate as ever. Lluckily the gig was recorded by Dave Lunt and recently was released as a CD on Document Records, nice it wasn't lost.

The success of the Booker gig gave Dave Lunt and myself the idea to do some more. So we started promoting gigs at Belle Vue, which was a little bit run down compared to when we used to visit the complex as kids. It sadly is no longer there at all now. It was first open to the public in 1836 and it closed its doors for good in 1987, lots of memories for many people are still vividly recalled.

We put concerts on every Wednesday at the Elizabethan Ballroom, the shows became known as Blues on the Park. These gigs rolled on until the middle of 1978 where we showcased amongst others, *Alexis Korner, Dick Heckstall-Smith, Zoot Money, Colin Hodgkinson, Tommy Tucker, Errol Dixon, Louisiana Red, Cousin Joe Pleasance* and many others, it was a great experience for us working as the house band in such a diverse field of artistes.

Alexis of course known as the Godfather of British blues was a great inspiration to us all, with his dedication to the blues. We were great friends, so much so he became Godfather to my eldest son, who is also called Alexis.

Eventually we moved from the Belle Vue venue as the Park was closing, so we carried on for a few more months at Rafters in Manchester's city centre.

The organisation of these nights took so much time and energy we were losing sight of what we were supposed to be doing, playing. It had been a success; we had made many contacts but it had to be laid to rest.

We had some very good memories of these shows, one of the many artistes we backed was a piano player and vocalist called Errol Dixon, who was Jamaican, but was explaining to us it's better if people think I am from the States for authenticity". So, we played along with it, but he gave the game away somewhat when he walked on stage in a Hawaiian shirt.

In many ways we have been very fortunate to be a small link in the long historic chain of original blues men and the forefathers of the genre. We appreciate it so much that we got to play with these legendary figures many who are sadly no longer with us. It's a pity that many young up and coming Blues musicians will never get the chance to meet these wonderful artistes. So, we try to incorporate some stories of these wonderful characters to keep the heritage alive for future generations.

We spent 1978 getting back to lots of gigging, and played with Alexis Korner, Johnny Mars and even had a residency at the legendary Band on the Wall in Manchester at weekends.

A concert I remember very well, and not the best memory either, was a gig we did at The New Theatre Drury Lane in London with Alexis. We were staying at a house that was so damp and dark it was horrible, it was a vacant property someone let us use in their absence. I could see why they didn't want to be there themselves.

Bob Brunning who was the first bass player with Fleetwood Mac and later the author of the book British Blues Connection came to our rescue and took us to his house for breakfast and a quick thaw out, most welcome.

We arrived at the theatre which has a 1,200 capacity and is very stylish. When we saw the PA we nearly wept. People have bigger speakers in their front rooms than the ones we had to use, and it looked even worse than it sounded as they were just sat on two Formica tables, we did our best to overcome it but it was not easy. It's really sad when a good concert is ruined by someone else's cavalier attitude to the sound.

We got a really good break, guesting on BB Kings October tour with Johnny Mars. This was the first time I had met BB, and what a wonderful man.
I remember asking him how it felt after years of struggling to suddenly be selling out Hammersmith Odeon for two nights, and he just replied 'Well every year we pick up another few fans" very modest, kind and a real gentleman.

I got to play in his band later on in Europe, and he told a newspaper "Norman is like a white Freddie King". I was so thrilled as Freddie was my absolute hero. It was a comment that has been quoted on all my biography's, of course ever since, it's the equivalent of By Royal Appointment' to a bluesman.

Chris Farlowe is always winding me up on stage (and the audience) when he says "As BB King said about Norman "WHO"? But it's an experience no one can take away.

On April 19th, we were invited to Alexis's 50th birthday party at Pinewood Studio on the set of The Great Gatsby, and what a night it turned out to be. Dave Lunt and myself had a great time. The whole thing was being recorded for WDR Television in Germany, well the main part anyway. On our arrival the first person I met was Dick Heckstall-Smith legendary saxophonist with Graham Bond, Colosseum and John Mayall to name just a few. We were good friends and I worked with him for many years with Jack Bruce.

We were gagging for a drink, so I asked Dick where the bar was, I was desperate for a beer. He was half way through eating a prawn sandwich as he pointed to the drinks counter while spitting crumbs trying in vain to tell me something. But my tongue was hanging out.

So being a good Northern lad I requested a pint of Bitter, the answer came back "Sorry sir, Champagne or wine only", I thought balls to this, so I asked for a pint of champagne. I think the barman had a fairly low opinion of me for some reason. Still, I was drunk quite fast so I didn't notice or cared very much.

Alexis fronted a great big band with various guests, myself and Dave among them, *Zoot Money, Dick Morrisey, Art Theman, Colin Hodgkinson, Mel Collins, Stu Spears (a wonderful drummer with the Meteors) later Chris Farlowe, Paul Jones, Duffy Power, Simon Kirke*, and many more.

When it came to my turn Alexis handed me his 1954 Gibson ES295 to play. I was soon to find out that it didn't work above the 8th fret but who cares it was the sort of night when anything wen., Eric Clapton turned up and played through any amp that was available no egos here just a great night spent with friends and musical brothers.

We stayed over at Boogie piano maestro Bob Hall's place and remember as we got the train home how pissed we all had been.

A friend of mine calls a hangover A negative reaction to a night out. Well, I was as negative as a newt, but what a great night, never to be forgotten, well most of it at least.

It was around this time I met saxophonist Lenni Crookes, best known just as Lenni. We were mates right from the start, great sense of humour and really over the top, but what a great player. He was playing with the top Manchester band Sad Café at this time, and I asked him if he was free to do a gig with No Mystery at a place called the Wilton Hotel in Swinton near Manchester.

We both liked each other's playing, until then anyway. It came to pass that on this day, there had been a beer strike, and all we could drink were bottles and all they had left was Carlsberg Special. Say no more, drunk, sick everything, but worst of all, we could barely stand up let alone play anything coherently. So, we both thought each other were crap. We still laugh about it to this day.

But we got over this alcoholic blip, gave it another try, and we played together for years, wonderful saxophonist, great showman too. He once sprayed his saxophone, metallic blue, and as he had some left over, decided to do his shoes too. More about Lenni later, too much to give you all at once.

We also became the first British Blues band to play in East Germany, or DDR as it was known. We did a Festival with Johnny Mars as a promotional show for the following years tour.

It was a real eye opener especially on the plane where pressurised cabins had gone virtually unnoticed by Interflug the state airline.
It was like having the bends when you came in to land, and there was a peculiar smell, like a sort of disinfectant.

The same year we did a couple of gigs with Jimmy Rogers. This was without doubt the hardest accompanying job I had ever done, and I've played with Honeyboy Edwards. Jimmy had just flown in that afternoon, so jet lagged he couldn't even tune his guitar. So, with no rehearsal we took to the stage, not one count in, not one key, not one song title it was playing absolutely blind. Jimmy was feeling pretty bad and asked me if I would take care of the solos and let him just play along and sing. No problem to me, it was easier than trying to work out what chords he was playing.

On one occasion I asked what chord it was, and he said "My fingers go here". Big help Jim.

Anyway, we somehow managed to get through the debacle, but worse was to come. The reviews of the gig were not great, and I was the main culprit as far as the critics were concerned for trying to upstage him, playing solos etc. Of course, they were unaware that it was what Jimmy had asked me to do. So, this is a very belated right of reply.

We continued through the year playing as No Mystery and with Victor Brox as guest on many occasions. We were also still promoting gigs on Wednesdays but this time back at Rafters on Oxford Road, Manchester.

As all musicians know however busy you are, it is not always matched with your earnings, so I was also playing a couple of restaurant gigs, which I really enjoyed for a change of styles. One of the restaurants was the Via Veneto in Manchester. One night who should walk in, knowing as you all do by now I'm a Manchester United fan it was Sir Matt Busby. Well that was it, no fear, straight up to him "Hi Matt how are you" etc. He was there with his wife to celebrate his wedding anniversary, the waiter is trying to get me away, I'm ignoring him and Sir Matt asked me to sit with them for a chat. What a gentleman. I bet he just wanted me to sod off, but you learn a lot about dealing with audiences from people like that, a true gent.

In 1979 and through our dealings with Johnny Mars we met his agent John Boddy, a real character. He used to look after a lot of the trad jazz gigs like Ken Colyer, Acker Bilk etc., but was now representing Johnny also.

We were invited back to tour in East Germany, it was all very James Bond and it was really exciting too. What an experience, a 16 date sell out tour. The gigs were magnificent, theatres, cinemas etc. we even got to meet some of the politicians of the time, as ambassadors.

The whole experience could turn into a book on its own. It was like Beatle mania, or Beakermania if you prefer. The audience never got the chance to meet, let alone listen to Western musicians live, we really were treated like Rock stars. The down side was, people were always after mementos of the west so anything not nailed down went in a souvenir hunters frenzy, not in a robbing way you understand as a collector's items.

It was strange for us to see the Inter shops where only Dollars or Sterling were taken, which of course meant the East Germans could only look longingly at things we take for granted such as toothpaste.

We travelled in a huge coach with an interpreter, Karlheinz Drechsel who was a renowned Jazz music journalist from Dresden who had been severely persecuted by the Nazis when they had turned against black music.

Each time we went past a factory or plant in the bus we were told to lie down on the seats so we couldn't be spying. There was even a curfew of 10.30 for lights on your vehicle so we drove with these interior little dim green lights as our only illumination. Very eerie, but as I said quite exciting we were experiencing first-hand the eastern bloc.

The people were wonderful, and in fact all of them were in work, no choice admittedly, but work, nevertheless.

The worst part was checking in hotels, I filled my passport up with visas in one tour. The hotel took your passports off you after the police had checked them, the whole process took ages, and was very tedious.

To crown the whole thing off, as we were returning home, Johnny Mars could not find his passport. It was like World War 3, no one leaves etc. Luckily it was in one of his bags, but it caused some consternation, and then a typical Victor Brox moment, he started to play his pocket cornet on the plane, to pipe Johnny aboard as it were. The airline staff did not see the funny side, nothing new there.

We were paid partly in sterling and mostly in Ostdeutsche marks. This currency was only worth anything in the GDR so we had to spend it there, which was a real task as everything was so cheap You could buy a meal for everyone in a hotel for about £10. Being tight northern musicians we would see a pair of fur lined boots for the equivalent of £8, and someone would say they had seen them for £7. I ended up buying an electric piano, a bass guitar and even an autoharp to use the money up.

Agent, John Boddy got on the coach one day and announced 'I have some good news and some bad. The good news is last night's show was recorded and will be aired tonight, the bad news is, you've been paid for it'.

It was probably the most remarkable tour for me, just because of the Iron Curtain thing, I learnt a lot more than a history book can teach you.

John Boddy was a real character, he was very dry, and used to say things like, "
'OK boys, lets lay back and relax, have a gin and tonic and put our feet in a bowl of warm water'. I called at his hotel room once and there he was large as life with his feet in water and a gin & tonic in his hand. We christened him Big Chief Few Beers as it was his favourite saying, we even bought him an Indian headdress and a pipe of peace to go with the name.

1979 was also a memorable time for reuniting with Jack Bruce for some gigs. There had been some contractual problems post Cream and it had limited what he could do musically for a while. Knowing Jack as I did, a lot of pent up musical emotion without an outlet is not a healthy combination, so I asked him if he fancied doing a few fairly low profile gigs just for fun, he jumped at the chance.

We played a fantastic first gig at the Band on the Wall in Manchester, the queue was all the way round the block, it was incredible. Jack was his usual fantastic self, and was without doubt the musician that influenced me the most.

We did a few gigs in Sheffield, Liverpool etc. and it was fantastic to see him back and firing on all cylinders. He was always a fiercely loyal friend and helped me many times over the years bless him.

He used to stay at my house, and we had some fun I can tell you. On one occasion, the shower was faulty so I told him to use the bath, but being Jack he took a shower, with water pouring through the ceiling in the kitchen. At a gig in Sheffield, he lost a front tooth and besides how it looked, he couldn't tell anyone to f… off, as it came out as flack. So, it became a catchphrase not giving a flack.

70's Morning After

1971 MORNING AFTER ALBUM

1975 with Dick Heckstall-Smith

Alexis Korner, Belle Vue1978
L to R Alexis Korner, Dave Lunt, Mike Smith and me

1978 With BB King Free Trade Hall Manchester.
Picture by Stewart Gunn.

Band on the Wall, Manchester 1979

EIGHTIES

We had been working so hard with No Mystery I was feeling a bit jaded and started to think I needed a break. My wife was offered a job in Belgium and we decided to move over there, probably for good.

It is always strange moving hook line and sinker to another country, but we rented our house out to a good friend of ours, so we had a safety net if we wanted to come home. Musically I was leaving quite a lot behind me but I needed a new challenge, and so off we went.

We had an apartment in Tervuren, a Flemish town about eight miles outside of Brussels. And within a couple of weeks, I met a drummer who lived in the same apartment block Ken Layton who invited me to a gig he was playing at in Brussels. I really enjoyed the band and within a month or two we had formed a band called **ABOUT TIME**. We used to play a mixture of my songs and the keyboardists Alex Smith who was an immediate interpreter at the EEC, and some Jack Bruce things. It was a lot of fun, and it was much more relaxed than I had been used to in Blighty. I came home occasionally to do a few Festivals with No Mystery so I still had my foot in the UK camp.

When I came back to Manchester, I used to borrow this old 1977 Fender Stratocaster, it was the first year they were made with a five position switch. It's a lovely guitar and it meant I didn't have to carry one backwards and forwards from Belgium.

I really liked it and when I came back for a Festival at Lyme Park in Stockport in June, my wife informed me she had bought it for my birthday.

It has a really original sound, sort of melancholy tone, it's very light too which is another bonus. It's looking worse for wear but so am I so we get along fine.

I loved Belgium. We met some great people, enjoyed the life style, everything, but a few months into this sojourn my wife found out she was pregnant, and understandably wanted to be near her own family. So, we came back to England in the August and I went back to No Mystery.

We started a residency at the Lamplight in Chorlton on a Monday night, and at the Band on the Wall in Manchester on Fridays and Saturdays. So, the calendar was pretty full with other gigs crammed in between.

It was at one of the Lamplight gigs that sax player Lenni was recording with Sad Café at Strawberry Studios owned by 10cc, and had been to the Waterloo pub opposite, and was a little bit tired and emotional. So, we escorted him from the studio in a stupor to the van which had a side door. We put his top half in the van and folded his legs up to his chest and locked it behind him. When we got to the gig, we opened the door and he fell out in the same position he had travelled in. We helped him up the stairs to the concert room, he got his sax out played brilliantly, and after the gig the same procedure in reverse and we dropped him off back at Strawberry.

The following day he said, "Something really strange happened last night, I had no money left after I had been in the pub, but found some this morning in my pocket, did I do gig?" Now that's a real beer moment.

1981 was a real eye-opener for me, my first child Alexis was born on March 8th. Nothing prepares you for a child around the place, and it takes some time to adjust. Equally I had to change my touring plans to accommodate a baby too.

Nick Franks the brother of Tim Frank's the drummer in No Mystery, was the owner of AMEK the world renowned mixing desk company, and he was also getting into managing a few bands. We were on his Radar what with family ties and all, so we recorded our first single for Nick's Jungle Telegraph label, "Taxman's Wine"/ "Doubt you Lord" and were lucky enough to get Ray Russel session guitar virtuoso to produce it for us and he made a beautiful job of it.

At this time, we had Balis Novak on keyboards. He had recently come to England from Lithuania, and quickly made a name for himself. He was a genius of player a wonderful musician, but he did have a bit of a drink problem, which made him a bit unpredictable and a little unreliable too.

We were playing gigs mainly in the North of England, Liverpool, Yorkshire that kind of thing so I could be home a bit more to help with the fatherly duties.

I started doing a bit of film extra and TV work at Granada to compensate for the lack of touring income. Extra work is a strange animal, hours sitting around doing nothing, then being asked to stay late to finish a scene. I even played a Rugby player in the TV series Fallen Hero, yes with my little legs!

I also did a couple of Cribb episodes, the Victorian detective series. There I was dressed up like Victorian waiter, cap, big shirt, apron and thick grey trousers, and guess what, some git hid my clothes for a joke, and I had to catch the bus home looking like Gilbert O'Sullivan's love child. Very embarrassing.

You meet some very strange people on the set, I must say, but a guy I met there who wasn't odd just very, very talented was a magician, memory man the lot, really amazing he was called Jack Steele. He impressed me so much I asked him to do some support gigs for us on some College dates, I thought it would be different, and that it was. Jack's main claim to fame was as a pickpocket, so on his first gig with us, he realised students have sod all in their pockets usually and no jackets to pick the pockets of.
So, he changed his act and actually started planting things on his audience like exotic condoms and the like, now that's what you call improvisation. He would produce all these rude artefacts and show them to the audience and hopefully the girlfriend was

rightly horrified at what her boyfriend potentially had in store for her. It was very funny.

Towards the end of the year, I met up with TV documentary composer by the name of Howard Davidson. He was also involved in a real mix of Blues and Cabaret with a band called the **State Rhapsody Orchestra** and he asked me to join, I couldn't refuse, it was a very interesting concept.

It was 1982, while recording with Howard Davidson for a programme called 2 Nations at the BBC Hippodrome in Manchester, I started to feel really feverish and unwell. It lasted all the following day and that night I was off to play a gig at the Philharmonic in Liverpool. My throat was really sore, and it was like a flu feeling. Anyway, I got through the night with a bit of a struggle but felt worse and worse. So, I called in the doctor, and he told me I had mumps, and was mystified how I had managed to sing the night before as all the saliva dries up. He checked the old tackle also, OK there but I was quarantined in the house for a week everyone had to move out. If I did venture out, I had to wear a scarf over my mouth so as not to infect anyone else. I had caught mumps as a child but apparently if you only have a weak bout of it, you can catch it again to finish it off.

No Mystery gigs were featuring a much changing personnel at this time and I started to think it was a bit unfair on the audience not to know who would be in the band and eventually, we didn't seem as committed as we had been. So, after a lot of thought we called it a day.

My wife was not thrilled about No Mystery splitting, as we had a child to bring up and it was a bit of a gamble, but the time seemed right to me.
We were all very proud of what we achieved with the band.

We stood almost alone in the Blues field for the first few years prior to, emergence The Blues Band, 9 Below Zero etc. and played a lot of gigs that were not always suitable for a Blues band but we were on a crusade, and we had a great time for years.

The next band project I got together 1983 reunited me with Lenni on sax and Tim Franks on drums, from the remnants of No Mystery, Howard Davidson on keys later Paul Kilvington, and Paul Allen on bass. Wee played all my own songs and this was called **Street Talk**, the first shoots of what was to become the Norman Beaker Band.

As well as playing my usual Blues gigs, with Victor Brox and Johnny Mars and Louisiana Red. I was asked to do a would be 60's Rock & Roll revue tour, with Tommy Bruce, who had hits with songs like "Ain't Misbehaving" Heinz who used to be in the Tornados and was famous for his tribute to Eddie Cochrane "Just Like Eddie", Wee Willie Harris who made a great record "Rockin at the 2i's" a tribute to the famous club and he really was the wild man of rock at the time. And last but not least Ricky Valence who recorded the hit I played at my talent show win in my teens "Tell Laura I love Her ".

It was a riot, the bass player Ted Lee, who sadly passed away in 2021, was one of the very top Luthiers in Britain he looked after my Fender Stratocaster for years. He decided in typical Ted fashion to come on stage stark naked, due to lack of excitement, his bass covered a bit, but not a lot.

Heinz was 'effing and blinding that he only ever got to sing Cochrane songs, Willie Harris didn't care about what he did. Ricky Valence sounded very American considering he came from Wales. He told me one time he would be at rehearsal 10 after one, we had to laugh.

At the last run through on the afternoon of the first show, Heinz had not appeared. All of the sudden he burst in panic stricken, his trade mark blonde hair had turned yellow at the hairdressers, what did he look like. All the way through the gig I couldn't take my eyes of this custard cut. I really enjoy these kind of things, the more outrageous the better.

It was a very sad start to 1984, after a short illness my close friend, mentor and Godfather to my son Alex, Alexis Korner passed away, it was a very sad blow to so many people who owed him such a lot.

We all thought he was on the road to recovery. In fact he sent me a letter just days before he died, hoping he would be out of hospital soon. He was a man who could advise you on anything and you listened.

Alexis was pretty much an atheist, but I remember a conversation he had with a Japanese guy who asked him why the British always won wars, and Alex told him, "It's because we believe in God". The Japanese guy said, "Well we believe in God too" and Alexis said "Yeah but how many Gods can speak Japanese".

When I first got some gigs in Italy offered to me, I asked him about the money situation, and he said, "Charge them double, and ask for half in advance". You can't buy that sort of advice.

On Friday 13th January a Memorial get together was held at Dingwalls, Camden Lock and some of the speeches were both poignant, some really funny. Jeff Griffin who produced Alexis's Radio 2 show was particularly moving.

A couple of years earlier while on tour Alexis agreed to do his Godfather bit in church for my son. It was quite an occasion, even the Vicar was impressed to have such a star in his midst. Bless him, Alex had carried a suit for the occasion for weeks while he was on tour.

My in-laws family were absolutely charmed by him, not seeming to recognize the cannabis leaf earring he was wearing, or that the cigarettes he was rolling, were not Silk Cut. But no matter, they thought he was great, as did everyone lucky enough to meet him. There are many stories about Alexis, and you can find out a lot from the brilliant biography written by Harry Shapiro.

My songs were becoming more sought after by other artistes, so in 1984 I signed a publishing deal with Pluto's Keith Hopwood who was one of the original members of Herman's Hermits and has many awards for TV themes and soundtracks.

I have always really loved song writing, it is a great feeling to compose something fresh, so I really got into that side of the business. I was also working with Jack Bruce again which was always a pleasure, and very cathartic.

A friend of mine received an Arts Council grant to record an album of local Manchester R&B bands. We were asked to submit a couple of tracks for the project that I had already recorded with Kevin Hill on bass who had been working with Victor Brox, Paul Kilvington keyboards, Lenni on sax and Tim Franks on drums. This was the real start of the Norman Beaker Band. Also, I had managed to edge myself into writing, performing and arranging jingles and TV themes such as Stand Up and the well-loved World in Action which was Granada TV flagship documentary programme.

1980 About Time

1987 with Lowell Fulson

1987 with Phil Guy

1988 KITE CLUB BLACKPOOL

1991 with Rufus Thomas San Remo Festival

NORMAN BEAKER BAND

After much deliberation I decided to call the band after my own name, not as an ego thing, but when trying to get gigs it helped to have a name that was recognised, and it also it meant if the personnel changed it wouldn't matter quite so much, so the **NORMAN BEAKER BAND** was born.

We were doing plenty of work and a lot of Festivals, which were a great shortcut to get through to a larger audience We had a set comprised of about 70% of my songs and the rest fairly traditional stuff but played with different arrangements.

We were really making headway but things don't ever run smoothly and my wife and I decided to split up. I was given custody of Alex who had only just started school. It was a very traumatic time, and it took me a while to get back to playing. Of course, organizing baby sitters was a big problem. However, Alex was an easy kid to have around, he got to see more blues festivals than anyone his age should have to endure. He used to occasionally comment, "What is that song everyone keeps playing" whenever another 12 bar shuffle was played.

If I had a gig abroad, I used to ask for the air fare money, and find a way usually by train to get Alex and myself there. One great occasion was a gig in 1991, when I was doing a festival in Salerno with Jack Bruce, Alex and myself took the train from London to Paris, Paris to Milan, stop off at Rome, then on to Naples where we were met by the tour manager. It took three days to get there then the gig and three days back.

The late great guitarist Alvin Lee of Ten Years After never forgot it, he was a great guy every time we met subsequently, he always wanted to know how long it took me to get there, it was a running joke. Just as an example of my useless sense of direction, I got lost in Rome walking round the Colosseum, yes, I know its round, that's what I mean.

In 1986 as the Norman Beaker Band, we recorded the Live album **"Bought in the Act"** which was recorded as the opening set on a Lowell Fulson concert who we were accompanying. It did really well, and the band now featured on keyboards the genius that is Dave Bainbridge, who later went on to form IONA.

This line up was to stay together for about 4 years. We were doing a lot of work for John Stedman again, the brains and owner of JSP Records, accompanying most of his US artistes, such as Phil Guy, Lowell Fulson, Louisiana Red, Carey & Lurrie Bell etc. touring and recording.

Phil Guy was very underrated, being Buddy's brother, it opened some doors for him, but also held him back I think. Phil was fantastic, a very aggressive player and vocalist and a great showman. The first time we met we really didn't hit it off, probably my fault. The gig was at the Band on the Wall in Manchester and I couldn't get there in time to rehearse, not my fault, but not the best start. I ran into the gig slightly late, plugged in my amp and guitar and started joining in. He looked at me and asked very bluntly what I was doing. I had to explain it was my band, so let's just get on with it. We didn't speak much that night, but I think it helped the gig, we were like 2 guitar slingers, it was a very exciting show. After the gig he came over gave me a big hug, and we were mates right up to his untimely death.

The following day we recorded a session for the BBC Radio 2 Paul Jones show at Strawberry in Stockport and it was really good. In fact, it came out on the "I Once was a Gambler" album on JSP the following year and has since been on countless reissues and compilations.

Phil was very funny. He also had a weird autograph, he used to write with the letters on their side going upwards very odd.

We used to play the odd trick on him, he wasn't very sure of the Sterling currency and he once said "If I put this down will I get a coke?" It was a 50p piece. I said yes but if you put some of the paper notes down, we can get some beer too, this he did, bless him.

I used to love playing with Phil, really amusing off stage but deadly serious on.

In 1987 As the JSP house band, we toured many times with the legendary **Lowell Fulson**. He was a very quiet and reflective man, bordering on the morose, but he wrote some great songs such as Tramp, Reconsider Baby, Black Night etc. We used to enjoy his stories especially the one about how Ray Charles stole his band off him, as Ray used to be in Lowell's band.

After a lot of gigs with Lowell on one tour, he was even more morose than normal, and we were all feeling a bit weary so I said to him Lowell will you cheer up for God's sake, he said look I'm really sorry, but my wife died a few months ago, and I have just been diagnosed with diabetes, it was one of the times you want the floor to open, and your mouth to shut, but I was so out there at the time I couldn't back down and came out with possibly the worst phrase ever, "I suppose you haven't got much to laugh about then", it's even worse when I'm writing it down.

I was very nice to him for a long time after that to make up for it. I think I was a bit bad tempered at this time, and nowadays would hopefully show much more tact and sympathy.

He worked a lot all over the world right up to his death in 1999 aged 77.

In March of '87 I was back in a relationship with a wonderful girl Dilys who was like a second Mum to Alex something I will always be grateful to her for. We were together for about 3 years but I felt she deserved more commitment than I could offer at that time. I met her again years later and she was happy and has two children of her own so I didn't feel so bad any more.

A strange phenomenon occurred about this time when I received a call from a guy called Mick Schofield in Blackpool. He asked me if I could do a gig for him at Blackpool Airport, in a sort of social club called the Kite Club. The money wasn't great, but he was so into blues and music in general it was impossible to refuse. There weren't many gigs in Blackpool for Blues, so I expected the worst. I couldn't believe it the gig was so full that people were outside standing on anything they could find and looking through the windows at the top of the building. It was amazing the enthusiasm and atmosphere that was generated was electric.

The first time I played there I wore a hooped sort of rugby shirt, which the audience must have thought was some sort of uniform, when we did a return gig a few months later everyone was wearing them audience and staff.

Now anyone who knows me will rightly testify to the fact, that I have never been at the cutting edge of fashion, in fact when I have tried to be it all goes wrong, I once bought a kaftan in the 60's this terrible orange paisley horror, I was so self-conscious, I tucked it in my trousers, what did I look like, don't answer.

The Blackpool gigs were getting such big audiences they decided to hold it at the Blackpool Winter Gardens. We were sharing the bill with some good friends of mine, Bare Wires.

It became the stuff of legends, and one I have been reminded of often.

The night before we had played at the Nottingham Beer Festival, which was absolutely jammed with expert revellers, so much so it was hard to get to the bar or the toilets. We had parked the van across the road from the venue, and there was a door at the side of the stage, which unfortunately and in total darkness, was a sheer drop of at least 10ft. I sprained my wrists my ankle, and dislocated my knee as well as cuts and bruises. Being an idiot and professional I somehow got through the gig in agony.

When I got home went straight to Stepping Hill Hospital, A & E department. I had to be taken for Xrays by wheelchair, they found that nothing was broken, but I was in severe pain. They gave me morphine to deal with it for the time being. So the following day we went to Blackpool for the gig, and the pain was getting worse and worse, but as I was already there, I had to do my best to get through the set. So stupidly I sent for a bottle of vodka, that I finished and added to the morphine was working a bit too well, at one stage in the set I tried to climb onto the Grand

Piano, absolutely off my face, then I played the intro to one of my better known songs, a sort of Jimmy Reed vibe, and after four bars fell backwards, I was lying on my back playing a different song, one of oldest friends Paul Gilchrist from Bare Wires, held me up until I'd finished the song. He has never let me forget it.

Ironically Blackpool being about fifty miles away from where I live, a local guy was at the gig and he came round to my house with a picture of the event. Always someone there when you don't want them.

I did manage to get compensation off the council for my injuries at least.

The fans at the Kite Club were amazing and the gigs ran for many years.

I played there in a duo with a friend of mine John Brett, and the reception was just as manic. Mick Schofield was also one of the artists that painted the illuminations, and it did not go unnoticed that one of the tableaux looked very like my band, T shirts with the Club and my face all over them were being sold on the famous Pleasure Beach, it was an unbelievable time, and a great club, it was a bit like Hitler's bunker but a better atmosphere.

The Club is still running today but at different venues, the original club was closed but the Kite was very special. Mick unfortunately passed away, but people have very fond memories of both him, the venue and the gigs themselves.

Another JSP artiste that crossed our path 1987 was **Rockin' Sidney**, a great Zydeco accordionist and singer, who wrote "Don't Mess with My Toot Toot" and "She's So Fine" as recorded by the Fabulous Thunderbirds.

This was very different style for me, coming from the more Chicago Blues side, so I was a bit stressed, after 1 hour of rehearsal for a live recording at the International in Manchester for yet another Paul Jones Radio 2 Show, I still remember it was the first time I felt really ill prepared, but we got through it with a certain amount of success thankfully, and the session which is out on CD "Paul Jones Radio 2 the American Guests Vol 3 tells its own tale.

Sidney was telling us how he used to see Elvis a lot on a Saturday evening, with his collar up, imitating the black guys going out for the night. His songs were great and he was a lovely guy, it was a very refreshing change for me a bit of Zydeco he did some good hoofin' too. and a great sense of humour that comes across in the lyrics. He sadly died in 1998 aged just 59.

The gigs and miles started to really mount up in 1998, we were touring constantly with an array of US stars, and now quite a few UK ones too.

We started doing some shows with **Paul Jones**, a really nice guy and a real aficionado of the Blues, even though many people still see him as a Boyish pop singer Do Wah Diddying everywhere from his Manfred Mann days. I've always liked Paul very much, and we did quite a few things together with songs of his choosing which gave him a bit more freedom possibly than the Blues Band and with a sax and keyboards we could choose a different slant and a variety of styles.

We did a very special concert in Kirkby- in- Ashfield in Nottingham, with Paul and **Colin Hodgkinson**, a really good friend of ours and a great source of jokes. He is a truly original player with a unique chordal bass playing style with a ragtime feel occasionally.

Although he plays as any self-respecting bass player should when he has to.

Anyway to return to the gig, we played a couple of songs then brought on Colin then Paul, and the place erupted, it was a wonderful night of good, solid blues and the audience which was huge absolutely loved it. Over the years Paul has guested several times with us and we always have a great time with him, alas he works so hard it's difficult to find a space in his or our schedule, but it's always been a pleasure.

Sometimes you win, sometimes you don't, a really good example of this was a gig we played at the Newcastle Jazz Festival, it was a night that seemed to last forever, and one of the most comical evenings I can recall. The business end however was different, we were to play in our own right, and later back the dynamic Boogie Woogie pianist **Katie Webster**, a truly great performer, we did it and it was all OK until the following night who was on, none other than Lowell Fulson being backed by the boogie, rockabilly Big Town Playboys with the great Mike Sanchez at that time. Shame it wasn't the other way round for all concerned.

The night belonged in no uncertain terms to the sax player who I have already mentioned, Lenni, boy he could get into some scrapes.

Breakfast at the hotel on the day of the gig should have warned me, Lenni saw Jeff Berlin world renowned bassist who had just flown in enjoying his breakfast, but not for long, Lenni in a good natured way took some sausages off his plate as he walked past his table. Jeff was gobsmacked, but we had a good laugh together about it later.

After the gig was over we decided to go and eat at a Chinese Restaurant nearby, the waiter ran past with a pan flambéing away, which alerted drummer Tim Franks to put it out with some water, cock up number one. We had all had a touch too much to drink, and dragged ourselves back to the hotel and decided we would have a late drink together, we switched on the TV to find a programme called "Naked Yoga", no explanation needed except, the voice over was none other than Alexis Korner, oh how we laughed as we dispersed to our various rooms after a good night that was had by all.

About 3am the phone rings, and a very distraught Lenni is on the line, almost in tears by the sound of it, very worse for wear, and not a little panicky "What's the problem" I enquired the chilling answer came back "I've lost my ring", I dare not go into what I was thinking, I ran down to his room to find him naked as a jay bird, his thighs were blood red, and there were three men prostrate on the carpet.

My God what's a boy to think. The aforementioned ring mystery was solved, it was one that his Mother had given to him and he treasured it but it had somehow come off in the bath and he was too pissed to find it.

So there I am rummaging away in his dirty bath water, I did finally retrieve it, he calmed down a little, and I thought it was time to investigate further about what had been going on, it came to light his legs were red from slapping himself in frustration, and trying to sober up a bit.

Now what about the three guys on the floor? He calmly told me, "Oh they are taxi drivers", like that was any explanation.

Anyway it appeared that he had a secret stash of alcohol which he gave to the first taxi driver who was then to drunk to drive so sent for his mate, same again, and then a third fell at the altar of Lenni's generous nature, three pissed up cabbies that had to stay in his room, thank God there was no YouTube then.

At last we were asked by John Stedman if we would like to record an album in our own right, we were certainly ready. I had a lot of songs I'd been working on for a couple of years, and a good selection of styles. It was very rare that a blues band played their own material so it was with some trepidation we set about the project.

We recorded the album at Cavalier studio in Stockport with the very talented and patient Lol Cooper engineering. We recorded and mixed it 5 days, and we were really happy with the result.

So feeling confident I sent a copy to John Stedman who said "I think we've made a mistake here, its a different sort of blues to what I expected". I remember feeling really dejected at first, but as soon as it was released and people really liked it, he changed his mind thankfully.

Even the cover idea was an accident, a friend of ours the late George Goode was going to do the photo shoot, and we had permission to use the Garrick Theatre in Stockport . It was just going to be us in front of the curtains, and this was going to be superimposed with a recording mixing desk. But the atmosphere didn't work, so we looked behind the curtain and found a whole Victorian living room set that was being used for the play showing there at the time.

It looked great and we took the shots right there and then, it fitted the title **"Modern Days, Lonely Nights"** in an ironic way. Especially when the photos were sepia tinted. Jack Bruce did the sleeve notes for us.
It was certainly a breakthrough album, and many bands played covers of the songs which was really pleasing.

Around 1989 I had reunited with Stockport multi-instrumentalist John Brett who played with just about every local band on the circuit, we were just mates playing blues guitars and having a laugh, but we weren't playing acoustic, we were rocking like a full band. John played great heavy Rhythm and some bass, and we started by accident to get loads of gigs, and offers of residencies, then some Arts Centre Concerts we had some great intimate gigs in the Bakers Vaults and later in the Crown Inn under the Viaduct in Stockport.

The Beaker Band were now pulling a lot of festivals too which seemed to me the best way to go domestically, less gigs more prestigious ones for more money. Kevin Hill who had been on bass up to this time had to give it up due to business interests, he was very instrumental in getting the band off the ground.

His place was taken by a young guy called Mark 'Chip' O' Connor, really great player I had seen him playing with a lot of local bands, he recorded quite a lot with us considering he was only with us for a couple of years, he can be heard on our **"Into the Blues"** CD on a couple of tracks also with Fenton Robinson, Louisiana Red, and Carey & Lurrie Bell.

Chip finally left to join the army, the following June, I don't know what that says about my man management skill's he preferred a Sergeant Major to me.

'Into The Blues' was the CD version of the 'Modern Days, Lonely Nights' vinyl. The CD had 4 extra tracks, two we recorded at the BBC with the late Dave Shannon who was the producer of the Paul Jones show at that time. These were the tracks Chip played on. The album did really well for us with 15 0riginal tracks.

We were to top the bill with **Fenton Robinson** at the first Burnley Festival, it was organised by Gary Hood who later repeated the success at Colne International Rhythm and Blues Festival.

Fenton had a very jazz oriented style, which for me me didn't quite work, but he had a great voice. We even did a blues master class on one of the days with him, which was one of the first I believe.

The show was televised, and put both Burnley and the Blues back in the limelight, and the festival ran with great success for many years.

NINETIES

So the search for another bass player to replace Chip was underway, I had someone in mind and that someone was **John Price**. John has been with me ever since, and the strange thing is, as with the rest of the band, I didn't ever ask any of them to join so I can't sack them either.

So without breaking stride we continued to record and tour in our own right and with visiting US stars such as **Lefty Dizzy** and **Byther Smith**, we were also appearing a lot on The Paul Jones Radio 2 show. Paul told me he used to get the odd complaint about how many times we were appearing, but it was just the way it was, there were not so many bands around at that time to accompany the many US artistes coming into the UK and word of mouth was getting us a lot of work. We owe his Radio 2 show a lot, due to the exposure we received from it.

In the February I was offered a Radio Show of my own with the local Station KFM, playing a mix of blues, soul and Gospel, I really enjoyed my time there, although at that time, we had to log all the songs we played by hand which was very time consuming. Through gigging with a lot of the Blues artistes.

I managed to secure some great interviews for the show, Buddy Guy, Jack Bruce, Charlie Musselwhite, Millie Jackson, Rufus Thomas, Kinsey Report, Joe Louis Walker, and many local bands too.

Jack Bruce, called at my house to come with me to the studio for an interview, but he knocked on the wrong door, when the occupier answered, he was playing a Cream album, and there at his door is Jack wearing a leather Hard Rock jacket looking all the world like a rock star, "Where does Norman live" he asked, the guy was gobsmacked and just pointed to my house, and Jack said "Thanks mate, nice music you're playing by the way ". I think the guy thought it was Candid camera.

We did the whole two hour show on Jack, which barely touched the sides as he had achieved so much, though one thing that used to get him mad was being in trivial pursuits as the question 'who was the third member of Cream after Eric and Ginger'

I really enjoyed doing the show, it felt like you were playing your favourite songs to your invisible friends, and I tried to promote a lot of local events too. My friend and occasional guitarist with the band Andrew Shelly used to engineer the show for me so I could concentrate on the presenting, and occasionally Andrew would do the show for me if I was unavailable.

We were again involved with the second Burnley Blues festival, which this year starred Buddy Guy, first time in the country for a long time, it brought a lot of kudos to the event. Buddy is a real character very amenable and funny. We also played with **Clarence Big Miller** for the first time at the Band on the Wall in Manchester it was quite a change in style for us. Much more jazz influenced, but a really big great voice.

The Jack Bruce tour with Dick Heckstall-Smith, was continuing and we had two shows in Greece. The first was in Thessaloniki, we had a really bad journey and only just made it to the venue in time, but just as we were about to take to the stage Jack disappeared, when he came back he was a very changed man and pretty out of it. When we got on stage it just got worse and worse, after a long , and I do mean long improvisation from Jack, Dick and myself, he staggered over to me to ask what song we were playing, not a good sign, and who will ever forget him saying to the Greek audience 'And they call this the home of civilisation eh' which didn't help much. It was a mess from the first song to the last.   The following night we played in Athens, and to be honest I was expecting much the same, but typical of Jack, it was a wonderful set, everything was perfect, when I spoke to him after the show, he said he preferred the night before, that was Jack for you, it was always a bumpy but incredible ride.

Lefty Dizz, obviously left handed, had a reluctance to change his strings, which he snapped more often than anyone I have ever played with, and never had a spare guitar so we spent a lot of time covering while he replaced them.

I remember a great night I spent in a jam session after the 2nd Burnley Blues Festival with **Angela Brown, Carey** and **Lurrie Bell**, and in fact the whole Bell clan including Steve, James and Tyson, they had been backing Buddy Guy and borrowed my keyboard player Dave Bainbridge who did not need to be asked twice, it was a hell of a party, and we played some great stuff.

I was also asked to do a radio session with the Jim Daley Band in Belfast, where things were a little tense at that time, Jim's band were the sort of equivalent of mine they were backing US artistes on the Irish gigs, they were a good band and had a great guitar player who I still see when we are in Northern Ireland Ronnie Greer, he's a legend in those parts.
We were also still playing quite a few shows with Phil Guy on his tour, which was always a lot of fun.

The band was working really hard and 1991 looked like that would continue, I also had a big European tour with Jack Bruce that was being put together. I was at Jack's house in Suffolk rehearsing when the news came on about the Gulf War and all that it entailed. So all the promoters were worried about insurance and travel arrangement, and the whole tour started to dissolve before our eyes. Eventually it was cancelled, we were not alone in this situation, many artistes had to cancel, not through fear, but as I said no one was willing to insure musicians flying all over the place.

This caused a lot of financial loss throughout the music business in general and I felt it in the pocket for sure as I had turned down 3 months of work to be free for the tour.

So from what looked like a really big year the future looked a lot gloomier. We did manage to rearrange some of the gigs later in the year however when the conflict had died down, but the damage had already been done.

During this hiatus I did a couple of shows with **Guitar Shorty**, very interesting guy he was known for his acrobatics as well as his guitar slinging.

On one occasion we played at the Redcar Festival at the Dome, it had been raining all day, so the stage was very slippery, this did not deter Shorty in the least, he took a run from the far side of the stage from me, and did an almighty somersault while playing, landed on his knees, and slid right past me on the waterlogged stage, and straight down the steps to the stage, it was really funny to us, but must have been very painful for him although he didn't show any lasting effects.

A music magazine reviewing the show kindly observed that 'Guitar Shorty was accompanied by Guitar even Shortier', nice. I have always enjoyed personal criticism if it's more about appearance than the music. The Melody Maker once said 'Beaker looks like a cross between Frank Marker and Columbo'. For those younger people Frank Marker was Private Investigator in a TV program 'Private Eye 'who always wore a grubby overcoat. The worst musical one I can remember was in NME music paper when I was about seventeen, and some critic I never would want to meet said 'He may not be the best Guitarist in the world, but he is certainly one of the worst singers'.
You need a thick skin for this job, but as Sibelius said 'No statue was ever erected in honor of a critic'.

Jack was putting some of the gigs that had been cancelled back on the schedule and one of the best ones was The San Remo Festival, set between Palm trees overlooking the sea, a perfect setting, the bill was really impressive too, Carl Perkins, Millie Jackson, Rufus & Carla Thomas, it was a great night.

We had to sound check early to avoid the enforced Siesta time, however the sound crew were running late, which didn't make Jack overly happy, so he just carried on anyway and started to knock out some Cream songs during the forbidden time of napping, it was hilarious, all the neighbours from surrounding apartments started screaming at us to shut up, at least that's what I think they were shouting, they threatened us with the police, so eventually he capitulated.

Rufus Thomas I had met several times, and I liked him a lot, and so did the fairer sex. A real character, I once asked him what he was going to wear and he said it's Blue. He came out on stage in what was a sparkling sky blue hot pants suit.

He was always very anti snobbery about black and white musicians, and never thought there was a difference be it blues or soul. An Italian Radio host interviewing him asked 'Do you only ever play black Music', to which Rufus stopped the interview and told him in no uncertain terms that he didn't play black music, he played music.

The host didn't quite get what he was talking about, so Rufus asked me to get him a pen so he could show him what he meant. So I handed him a pen and looking the interviewer in the eye, without looking at what he was writing, he did a stave with some notes on it and handed it to the guy. He said "Ok there is some music, what colours do you see? the guy replied Red and White, Rufus looked at me and said "Shit, wrong pen".

While I was in San Remo I was getting everyone to do interviews, and some celebrity trailers for my radio show. I asked Millie Jackson and she said, yeah no problem, "Listen to Norman Beakers show or I'll f......g kill you". She did eventually do one I could use, she was so feisty but great fun.

We drove back to Nice airport to fly home, and while waiting, who should walk in the lounge but Ringo Starr and his wife Barbara Bach. I heard Barbara say "Ask him" so he turned round to me and enquired where and with whom I'd been playing, I told him with Jack Bruce , and he said "Where is Jack"? I pointed him out, Jack was flat out lying on some chairs, and he said "That's the same pose as the last time I saw him at Eric Clapton's wedding".
Ringo has always been a great guy, with as much enthusiasm now as ever. Jack worked many times in later years with Ringo's All Stars.

In the September of 1991 the Radio Station I was working for sold out to Signal in Stoke, and my show like many were replaced with more middle of the road music, but I had really enjoyed the experience and it helped me when I was being interviewed, seeing it from the other side really good experience.

I always seem to get childhood diseases later than anyone else, so feeling a bit unwell I went to the doctors to find I had Scarlet Fever, I was always told when I was a kid you caught it messing about near drainage grids. I felt dreadful, but everyone kept telling me that I looked great with a good tan, don't believe what you see.

About this time 1992 the legendary Dick Heckstall-Smith had heart surgery and was really having a bad time financially too, so a mutual friend of ours Richard Everett who was the leader of the Sensational King Biscuit Band organised a benefit concert to raise a few quid for him on 2nd June at the 100 Club in Oxford Street London.

It was a great night, I played with Micky Waller on drums, Paul Jones on harp, Bob Hall and Zoot Money on keys, and the wonderful Dick Morrisey and Art Theman on saxes. I had a great time, it was recorded on a video called "100% Blues."

On the subject of benefits, I was the recipient of one myself, I had developed nodules on my vocal chords, a very tricky operation voice wise, but it is a bit of an occupational hazard singing Blues. Probably made a lot worse as the harm had been done before the smoking ban in clubs became law, it's so much better for singers since the ban.

The wonderful Blues fraternity thought I could do with a few quid to tide me over the convalescence of the op which can take a while. And straight away Jack Bruce, Tony McPhee of the Groundhogs, Helen Watson, the late Paul Young of Sad Café & Mike and the Mechanics and a host of local bands offered their services. Even Granada TV did a clip of me trying to sing, to promote the show.

There is a definite bond between musicians that hit hard times, most of us have or will do at some times but there is a kind of brotherhood who look out for each other just out of respect for

91

their own people, quite often in secret from the public not for publicity but purely because they want to help.

The day of the operation had been set for the beginning of December and the Concert for 14th, however I got a bad case of flu and the operation was put back until the New year, so I actually attended my own bash, and even played at it, I was very touched by everyone's concern.

Finally, 13th Jan 1993, after being postponed twice I had the nodule removed, it was not so unpleasant, but I also had nasal polyps removed at the same time, which in retrospect was not a good idea. I couldn't speak or breathe properly, also the outcomes on the vocal chords op vary, thankfully I was one of the lucky ones, all I have had to do to compensate is to lower a few keys now and again.

People who know me, realise I'm a bit of a chatterbox to say the least, so it was so difficult to communicate, and everyday chores were really difficult, it makes you realise how difficult being deaf or mute must be.

I had worked out a system with my son Alex who's bedroom was opposite the stairs, so that if the phone rang, I would throw a tennis ball at his door to alert him to answer. Great idea, except the first time I tried it, I threw the ball it hit the door, bulls eye, Alex comes to the door and asks "What do you want". grrrrr
I remember during this time one Sunday morning, when the wonderful Charlie Watts phoned me about the Alexis Korner Tribute gig and my son Alex answered the phone, the conversation went like this, " Hi its Charlie" - Alex "Charlie who", "Charlie Watts," what do you do, asks Alex "I'm the Rolling Stones drummer", Alex cooly said "You will have to ring back when my Dad can speak".

Charlie sadly passed away on the 24th August 2021 aged 80. He was a wonderful kind man, everyone quite rightly loved him, and a fantastic drummer too.

Alex also at this time told Robert Stigwood I was on the toilet and told him to ring back, I wouldn't have minded so much but I was in the kitchen.

After the op I wasn't allowed to speak at all for at least 2 weeks, and under no circumstances was I to try to clear my throat or whisper.

No alcohol for 2 weeks either, so on the fifteenth days after post op, a beer would be like cake to a starving man. Not being able to speak I decided I would get a couple of cans from the off licence. I had the correct money ready so no talking was necessary. I went to the counter to pay, put the cans down gave her the money and she said "Anything else". I shook my head. She continued "there are some good deals on if you want". Again I shook my head, and a woman in the queue behind, me asked very kindly "Are you alright love", I just nodded and walked out. I still wonder what they thought was wrong with me.

Not being able to clear my throat was really difficult. Initially it felt like a breadcrumb was stuck in my throat. The only way I could soothe the itch was to sort of exhale quite forcefully to create a breeze over the affected area. Unfortunately it made a very effeminate noise as I did it which alarmed many, and certainly myself.

Anyway, my voice returned over a period of months, and I was anxious to get back playing, so after 3 months I did a gig at Mansfield Art Centre a nice little venue I knew well. But I had a guest singer George Phillips from Bare Wires to lighten the burden just in case.

It was strange, I felt really nervous. It was probably the longest gap I ever had between concerts, and it was not a very auspicious start I'm afraid.

I walked on stage greeted the audience and my guitar strap came off, the guitar hit the ground with a hard thud and made this frightening mixture of twanging and feed back noise. What a din! So out of embarrassment I told the audience, it was a trick I learned from Jimi Hendrix, but I didn't have a lighter to set fire to it unfortunately. The audience laughed probably at and with me, but I was back in the saddle and felt good and comfortable back on stage.

The spring time has always been a busy time for us, both as accompanying other artistes from the USA or in our own right doing the Jazz & Blues Festivals, this year was no different.

We were booked to play with Randall Boykins and the wonderful **Larry Garner** at a few shows over the Bank Holidays, we did a Paul Jones Radio session with Randall on the way to Portsmouth to do their Blues Festival.

The weather was really appalling, the winds were very strong. We played on the Saturday, luckily as the following day, the marquee blew down, and they had to move the whole thing to another place which did not help Heineken the sponsors to recoup much of its sponsorship outlay.

Meeting Larry Garner again was a real pleasure, I have always admired his playing, his voice and his song writing, and of course his story telling. He was obviously going to be a big star. He had been recording for JSP like ourselves but got a big deal with Polygram and made several big selling albums.

We played a lot of Festivals this year, one of my favourites was at Newark, we were appearing with Georgie Fame. I have always been a massive fan of Georgie, so it was nice to see him close up. I also remember his sax player the legendary Alan Skidmore who hid the Gold trumpet belonging to Guy Barker, who wasn't overly amused.

I had for many years been involved in booking artistes for festivals and this year I was booking the Edinburgh Blues Festival to run alongside the well-established world renowned Jazz Festival.

We played with Johnny Mars and Paul Jones and it was a lot of fun, especially as the venue was the Caledonian Brewery, and the dressing room was the tasting room too. Needless to say. the party went with a swing, and goes to disprove the old story of not being able to run a piss up in a brewery, this was one.

Later in the year we had the privilege of backing **Carol Fran** and **Clarence Holliman** at the Colne Municipal Hall. We had never met before, and only had one album to learn the songs from, but they didn't do any of them. What made matters worse, they were late getting to the venue, and we were on stage to keep the show moving along until they arrived. So, without even having chance to say , Carol gets on the piano, first song "Rain or Shine". Clarence, Carols husband and a very fine guitarist, were shouting the chord changes to everyone throughout the whole set, which somehow worked perfectly, I think someone up there was on our side.

It was a lovely gig, and the following day we did the Paul Jones Radio 2 shows live session. This time we actually had a chance to talk and work the songs, and it was a fantastic session, Clarence was a great bandleader, unfortunately he died in 1994.

After the Radio session Carol gave me a big hug and I disappeared into her ample bosom, and Clarence shouted "Hey Norman get your ass out of there". Really nice couple and a pleasure to be in their company.

It was now 1994 ten years since the death of Alexis Korner and as the man himself loved to do, we decided to ask a host of musicians to appear and put a Memorial Concert together at Buxton Opera House in Derbyshire, a beautiful 1000 seater Edwardian theatre. It was fairly easy to get the first few names down, like Colin Hodgkinson, Zoot Money, Dick Heckstall-Smith, Chris Barber etc.
However, when news got around everyone wanted to do the show, how were we going to fit it all in, we only had five hours.

It was wonderful all these names from the past were on the phone, and people like Charlie Watts, and John Mayall were contacting me to apologise for not being in the country at that time to perform. The list was getting slightly frightening, and

95

then a call from **Robert Plant** who of course used to work in a duo with Alexis confirmed he wanted to do it. Robert is truly one of the good guys in the business, and he still has the same attitude now he had when he started. The list kept growing, I was trying to pair musicians up to get through the list, it was very exciting but needed a lot of planning.

Then out of the blue came a call from Robert Plant, "Would it be OK if **Jimmy Page** did it with me?" Well I wasn't ever going to say no, was I? So they were going to be on stage together again for the first time in about 15 years. This goes to show the amazing influence Alexis had on everyone.

The date was Sunday April 17th. I hadn't slept much worrying about the lack of rehearsal time. I had made a running order and that was about it, but it appeared that everyone was going to get about 10-15 minutes each, which as Robert said was "a bit of a tease", but we did manage to let him and Jimmy have 20mins.

Bob Harris was co-compere for the event alongside the late Dave Shannon who was the producer of the Paul Jones Radio 2 show and guitarist with the folk band Therapy. Pete Johnson from Key 103, Jazz FM and BBC2 Producer was interviewing and doing some of the introductions too.

The rehearsals were very short, with such a lot to get through, but the show only overran by five minutes in five hours, due to the strict stage management of one of the organizers Harry Lee.

As with Alexis we too wanted to give a break to up and coming bands, and on this occasion two songs from the Winchesters a Western Swing type band got the show up and running. I cut my set to two songs as I was playing most of the night, as indeed was John Price on bass, Tim Franks on drums Dave Bainbridge on keyboards, Lenni on sax and Andrew Shelley on slide. We decided to put Robert and Jimmy on to close the first half, this they did with great aplomb and the atmosphere was really electric.

And it was obvious the audience were there out of respect for Alexis too.

The bill was as follows, *The Winchesters, John Pearson, Raphael Callaghan & Christine Purnell, Bob Hall, Duffy Power, Davy Graham, Dick Heckstall- Smith, Art Theman, Dick Morrisey, Pete Brown, Colin Hodgkinson, Herbie Goins, Guido Toffeletti, Zoot Money, Paul Jones, Victor & Annette Brox* Chris Barber, *and Umberto Saachi.*   One moment I remember, from the first concert was the look of disbelief on this guy's face who was staying at the same hotel as all the artistes, The Palace, which was opposite the venue. He wondered what was going on. He was a true Blues fanatic who knew nothing about the show, so to be sat in the lounge with Robert Plant & Jimmy Page etc. was overwhelming him. He begged us for two tickets, but they had all gone months before.

He was so distraught we were trying to find any way we could accommodate him. There were already over two hundred people backstage including artistes, but in the end, we couldn't say no. So, we put strict instructions on him that he had to sit on a flight case in the wings and not move, and this he did for about 5 hours. I bet his backside was sore for weeks, but it was so great to help someone have the night of their life.

Now that was quite a show. Alexis's widow Bobby attended and had a wonderful evening and was presented with flowers on stage, which was very moving. She sadly passed away in 2021.

It was run as a charity event in aid of McMillan Nurses.

We decided due to the success that maybe we should make it an annual event, and so we did for the next nine years. They were wonderful shows though I say so myself. There were many ups and downs putting these shows together, when people who were available one day, had no choice but to pull out later, but mainly they were very good times.

Later in the year, flush with success from the Alexis evening, we decided to put a Buxton R & B Festival on and involved a few more people to help put it together. This was a good case of running before you can walk, it was musically great but financially ruinous. Sometimes when you are a player yourself, you have your own ideas who's popular and can draw crowds, and it was to my considerable cost we got it wrong. It was a lesson well learned, and never to be repeated, unlike the Alexis Memorial shows.

1995 was to become a really eventful and busy time, it was also the start of a long musical collaboration with **Chris Farlowe.**

Chris one of the finest vocalists the UK has ever produced, with a career lasting over sixty years. He is probably best remembered for the timeless number one hit "Out of Time" which was written by Mick Jagger and Keith Richards, and produced by them.

Although not as big as Out of Time, he recorded the definitive version of "Handbags & Gladrags" which was written for him by Mike D'abo of the Manfred's. The song has been covered by Rod Stewart and the Stereophonics, and has been used as the theme for the Ricky Gervais comedy "The Office" but many still prefer the original. It's a song I have always enjoyed playing live.

But these hit records are such a small part of his lengthy, legacy he has relentlessly toured Europe since the sixties worked with Jimmy Page on his Outriders album, appeared with Otis Redding on a Ready Steady Go as his special guest, and is admired by the major rock singers such Roger Daltrey, the late Joe Cocker, Robert Plant, Van Morrison and even Lisa Minelli and Tina Turner.

It was while playing with Chris at the 2nd Alexis Memorial Concert that the idea of pairing him with our band came from Del Taylor who was in the process of signing Chris to Indigo Records.

Del was long time manager of Alexis Korner and was busy putting an artiste roster together for the label and Chris was high on his list. He then asked me if I would be interested in producing the album which was to be a live one, with my band on the session.

Didn't take long to say yes, and we have worked together with some gaps due to other commitments ever since and we have seen a lot of the world and had a lot of fun together.

The first gig we played together was the recording of the live album at Salisbury Art Centre on the 15th July. We had just one day rehearsal (which is one day more than we often get) and then recorded the show the night after.

It could have gone either way with little room for error, but it worked really well. Unfortunately, my long-time drummer Tim Franks was busy on another venture as was Dave Bainbridge, so Paul Burgess of 10cc, Camel, Jethro Tull etc. took over on kit and Dave Baldwin from Icicle works joined on keyboards.

This was a defining moment as we were fast becoming the house band, with Del and myself producing the sessions. So, we didn't see much of Tim after that as we were working so much with Chris, who likes to keep a stable band as much as possible. So, the band was now, Paul Burgess drums, John Price bass, Dave Baldwin keys, Lenni sax and myself.

The album "**Lonesome Road** " was very well received and it was obvious right away we were a strong partnership, and things just worked. It doesn't happen too often, although we have very different personalities, musically we were very together.

The Alexis Memorial live album was also released on Indigo, which this year featured Jack Bruce playing a great set with us, and a memorable duet about Sonny Boy Williamson with Paul Jones. The rest of the bill was *Micky Moody, Bernie Marsden, Zoot Money, Tony McPhee, Colin Hodgkinson, Jimmy Litherland, Dick Heckstall-Smith, Mick Abrahams, Brian Knight, Tony Vines, Dave Berry, Brian Wood, Ray Warleigh, Alan Skidmore, Blues Shouter, Herbie Goins, Mike Sanchez, Andrew Shelley, Chris Barber Umberto Sachi,* and from my band *John Price, Tim Franks, Dave Bainbridge and Lenni.*

The albums were released as a 3 CD set. Even the mixing of this event was fraught with danger, as there were microphones all over the stage, with huge personnel at times. Luckily, we had a video of the show, so I had visual assistance to tell me which mics people were on, and in fact who that someone was.

It only took two days, to mix but it seemed longer. Jack Bruce said he thought it sounded great, and asked who mixed it, I proudly told him me, and he said, "well it's not bad anyway".

Every year the Alexis Memorial gigs took months to organize, always trying to be true to the memory of Alexis, and what he stood for.

We were always trying to obtain the services of big names who were connected either musically or through friendship with Alexis, and so it did not become just another jam session.

It was a sad time too when Rory Gallagher, a good friend of ours and one of the most popular blues guitarists the UK has ever produced, tragically passed away.
I had a great time interviewing him on Dec 20th 1990 at the Grand Hotel in Manchester prior to his gig at the International. It was a lot of fun, instead of an interview it became just two guitarists reminiscing. It was very refreshing. The interview was for KFM Radio in Stockport, and so it was a big deal for all of us at the station.

Rory was of course always loved by Blues fans, but his death has made him into a true icon, and rightly so. Everyone who met him could not fail to find him charming and humble, a true blue genius. Of course, his legacy is great, and annually there are many conventions and Memorial gigs in his honour.

In fact, we organised a tribute gig ourselves very much on the same lines as the Alexis Concerts in the October of 1997, which I will come back to later.

In January 1996 and before the work tornado blew in, I managed to find time to get married to Wendy, or Long suffering

Wendy as she was once called on a Chris Farlowe album, what can they mean.

The recordings for Indigo carried on at a pace in 1996, when I recorded and produced **Mick Abrahams** album **"Mick's Back"**
Mick was a founder member Jethro Tull and Blodwyn Pig. We had a lot of fun doing this album together, Mick's a great guitar player, and I took quite a back seat approach to this as there was no need for a lot more guitar, so I concentrated more on arrangements and production.
The album was made up of standards and original compositions, but all given the Abrahams treatment.

The next album on the production line was with the wonderful **Ruby Turner**, now an MBE who I had long admired. She was a pleasure to work with and the resulting album **"Guilty"** is still one of the albums I am most proud of. The material was very varied from the Beatles to Brook Benton, Jools Holland played piano on a few of the tracks too.

I don't think I had ever had so much going on at the same time, here is a glimpse of the schedule in March alone
1st-5th, Recording backing tracks for the Ruby album at Frog Studio in Warrington
8th-17th Touring with Chris Farlowe
18th-20th, Recording Ruby's vocals at UB40's Dep studios in Birmingham,
23rd-30th Touring with Chris Farlowe .

This sort of schedule went on throughout May including the third Alexis Memorial Concert. This year featured, amongst others. *Peter Green, Paul Jones, Mick Abrahams, Andy Fairweather Low, Chris Farlowe, Ruby Turner & Bernie Marsden.*

It was a real coup to get Peter Green back on stage. He was always one of my favourite guitarists, as indeed he was to most players. His solos were always a thing of taste and beauty. He had a lot of mental health problems which is well documented, but I was so pleased to see him again however fragile he appeared. He wasn't musically at his best after a long layoff, but just to have him back in the fold was wonderful. He continued to record several albums after this night with the Splinter group. Of course, he was a wonderful songwriter too, with extremely poignant lyrics.

The beginning of 1997 brought a new Chris Farlowe album entitled just **"The Voice"**, it was produced by Clem Clemson of Humble Pie and of course an ally of Chris's in jazz rock band Colosseum.

We recorded for a week, and it was to be the coldest week I ever remember. The studio was freezing, we couldn't find Chris in the amount of clothing he had on. We all had our coats on, Clem with a scarf, not ideal weather for recording, but it got done just the same.

Ricky Byrd guitarist singer from Joan Jet's band wrote and played on a couple of tracks. He was a really nice guy, we had a lot of fun, but even as a recovering punk, he found English humour, and especially mine a bit earthy. **Elkie Brooks** performed a duo with Chris on the classic "Private Number".
It was a fine album with keyboards from Ronnie Leahy who I had worked with before with Jack Bruce.

This was also the year we toured Germany, Switzerland and Holland with Chris as a whole band for the first time, and was really enjoyable. We did 18 shows.

On the domestic front my second son Joel was born, on 4th Feb so it was a big change again, I had forgotten how much work there is involved, as it had been 16 years since my first son was born. But work carried on at full tilt.

The Alexis Memorial came around it seemed more quickly every year, and this year the quality was just as good with, **Tim Rose** who was a good friend of mine for many years, *John Pearson, Bernie Marsden* who always wanted to play at this gig,

Chris Farlowe, Victor Brox from my old days, *Dick Heckstall-Smith* and *Ian Hunter* of Mott the Hoople.

We had changed the artistes as much as we could, but we were starting to repeat a few, and so we put artistes on the bill who had maybe not directly played with Alexis but owed a lot or had been inspired by him.

We also put a tribute concert on in memory of Rory Gallager, again at Buxton Opera house, at the request and assistance of Rory's brother Donal who was also Rory's manager. The concert took place Oct 5th a couple of years since his passing. This featured *Paul Jones,* the amazing *Lonnie Donegan, Tim Rose, Peter Green and the Splinter group, Ronnie Drew of the Dubliners, Bernie Marsden, Marie Ni Chatasaigh and Chris Newman,* and ourselves the house band.

Van Morrison was due to appear, but unfortunately was taken ill a couple of days before, but he made a generous donation to the charity involved.

It was a wonderful night. We had Rory's Fender Stratocaster on stage for the whole night. Bernie actually played a few songs on it, with permission of course.

It was a more solemn concert than the Alexis ones as it was so near to his death, but I think we marked his passing with a bang and hoped that he would have enjoyed it. I know Donal did.

On what seemed to be a very rare night off in a local pub I saw an amazing collection of musicians called Rubber Zoo. They were on the same planet occupied by Frank Zappa. They were great musicians, really original. So, I had a word with Kris Gray, then manager of Chris Farlowe, and he put some money together to record them, with me producing. I think I learned a lot more from them than they did from me.

It was an experience on both sides. Unfortunately it never saw the light of day even after a few gigs with Ian Hunter of Mott the Hoople, who really liked them. It was just so hard at that time to get plays and venues to give it a try and it sort of fizzled out. A great shame as far as I was concerned, a chance wasted I thought.

We started recording my next album the **"The Older I Get the Better I was"**, at Frog Studios in Warrington, with Tim Duncan engineering. We worked together on the Ruby Turner and Mick Abrahams albums.

We always worked well as a team. He is really fast at getting the sounds I want and it helps to keep the momentum and intensity high.

This album was very song based, not so may big solos and straight ahead Blues, although it does have some of that of course. I had so many songs written and I had to get them out while I still liked them.

It was a band album with Tim Franks on kit again, John Price bass, Dave Baldwin keys and Lenni saxes, John Hulme on trumpet, Clive Mellor guesting on harmonica and Sheila Gott on backing vocals, again.

Sheila struck up a great partnerships with Ruby Turner Mick Abrahams and Chris Farlowe. It's always good when you have a pool of musicians you respect and are comfortable with. It is so much faster and less fraught.

I remember these sessions for many reasons mostly they were good fun. I remember the look on Clive Mellor's face when he had finished his contribution to "Standing on Shaky ground" which incidentally was about this woman stalking me, before I even knew what stalking was, quite a weird feeling that. Clive had to play a really fast rhythm pattern on harmonica, his lungs must have been ready to burst. He came out of the studio looking like a tomato, I could not resist asking him to do it again. It was a joke as he got it first time perfectly, lucky for him.

As I was putting down the vocals with Sheila, the sad news that Princess Diana had been killed in a car crash in Paris, broke.

It was very strange to see the public outpouring of grief, I'll never forget the general atmosphere over those first few days. It seemed to move public grieving to another level, and it has become a normal ritual now.

The album was a mix of Blues, Rock ballads and even some funk, and it did really well for us. It was released on Kris Gray's Citadel Label.

On Fri 13th February 1998 my third son Nathan was born. He couldn't wait for St. Valentine's day, so Friday 13th it was.

The workload was not letting up for Paternity leave, so in March we embarked on a UK tour with Chris Farlowe, which ran for the whole month. It finished just before the 98'Alexis Memorial Concert. Eric Bell of Thin Lizzy did his stuff with John Coghlan of Status Quo on drums, and Noel Redding legendary bassist with the Jimi Hendrix Experience.

A highlight for me that night was playing with **Jim McCartey** and **Chris Dreja** of the Yardbirds. Remembering all those years ago it was the Five Live Yardbirds album that really turned me on to R & B, and the wonderful **Mark Feltham** of Nine Below Zero fame on harmonica, filling the shoes of the late Keith Relf. who sadly died in May 1976 from electrocution while he was playing electric guitar. I was really in Blues heaven with Jim doing most of the vocals, it was really a dream come true for me.

Another of my heroes I got to play with on this particular night was **Colin Blunstone** of the Zombies. They have always been a favourite band of mine, and Colin was superb, we played the usual hits, "Time of the Season", "She's not there" and "Say you Don't Mind" a lot rockier than his original hit version of the Denny Laine classic.

Whenever we meet up with the Zombies we always have a wonderful time, and love listening to each other.

It never ceased to amaze me how so many people from very different genres of the music scene all felt they owed such a lot to Alexis. Bob Harris who compered many of the shows, was so pleased to be there as Alexis had been there for him at the beginning of his radio career, and also Tom Robinson, who performed a wonderful acoustic set, spoke of how inspired he had always been from his meetings with Alexis, quite a legacy.

Other artists performing at the concert were Colin Hodgkinson, Hilton Valentine and John Steele of the Animals. Aynsley Lister was the new kid on the block then, but was even then a great act, Bernie Marsden and Micky Moody, and one of my best mates the late and to me the very great **Tony Ashton**. Known mainly for his number 3 hit Resurrection Shuffle with Ashton Gardner and Dyke. Tony was a wonderful keyboardist and contributed to so many albums. He was such a good spirited, kind, crazy man. The place lit up when Tony was around.

At his funeral so many people eulogised about him that it was almost too late for him to be buried. The stories people told about Tony especially one of his closest friends **Jon Lord** of Deep Purple, were bringing tears of joy and sadness in equal measure.

Jon and Tony used to love going to Zermatt in Switzerland. He recalled the time when he and Tony were on a mountain top, looking at the beautiful snow peaked scenery, and Tony just looked up to the heavens, and said "Nice one God "
He was so much fun, the late Long John Baldry who Tony worked with on and off for many years, once told him, not to bring beer on stage as it didn't look professional, Tony liked a medicinal pint for sure, in fact if his mind ever went blank, he used to refer to it as a Lager moment.

Baldry who used to be known amongst musicians as Big Jack Bradley, cracked up when Tony said "I'm being very professional, beer is my act".

On the Alexis concerts we had a few drummers, bassists, guitarists and so on, but on this night just two keyboard players Dave Baldwin and Tony. He convinced Dave it would be nice to go for a pint. Of course Tony was enjoying himself, and they only just made it back to the theatre on time, after a lot of panicking from yours truly. We decided in future to follow the protocol of the Royal Family, always keep one in reserve, don't have everyone in the same car together.

Tony Ashton sadly died from cancer on 28 May 2001 at his home in London. He was 55.

Shortly before his death, he sent this message.

Dear everyone,
Thanks for all the messages and enquiries,
recent tests show the cancer has spread
and I've decided to refuse further treatment and come home.
So-thanks to all, have a drink for me-cheers and
*   bollox...*
- Tony Ashton.

Another great player lost to us in 1998 on 5th April was a real shock to everyone when **Cozy Powell** one of the most loved and respected of all fellow musicians and one of the most prolific drummers in the business was killed in a car crash. His CV runs like a Who's Who of rock. I knew him for many years, and his enthusiasm was endless, he was always up for a play or a jam, and it was always a pleasure to meet up with him, a truly great guy, and so laid back

We were still touring a lot with Chris in 1999, and one of the gigs we played was in Antwerp and it was amazing. The show featured so many artistes from 50s 60' and 70s. We all played a couple of songs set up on a revolving stage, and we all travelled on the same coach, with many people I had never met before.

Marty Wilde, Alvin Stardust, The Tornedos, Racy, Clem Cattini, Showaddywaddy, Swinging Blue Jeans, Paul Jones and the Manfreds, Rubettes the list was endless.

But I loved meeting up with these guys we had a ball. The promoter must have known what might happen, with Belgian beer on tap, and so they refused to serve any artist until he had performed. We were praying to be on first.

Dave Bartram lead singer of Showaddywaddy sat in front of Chris Farlowe and myself, and Chris was complaining about us only playing two songs, and they were doing about four. Dave turned around and replied "probably because we've had 22 top ten hits and you've had two". No coming back from that one then.

We were asked to put together a Memorial gig to Cozy Powell. We agreed to do it the day before the annual Alexis one, on May 1st and 2nd. It was hard but rewarding work.

We were as usual putting both of them on for charity, and we were looking for something to raffle, and we came up with the idea of a presentation of a collection of drums sticks from various well known drummers set in a frame, by a local picture framer Steve Wilson.

It looked brilliant, signed sticks from Mick Fleetwood, Ringo Starr, Pete York, and many more. The show was amazing, Spike Edney keyboard wizard and bandleader, introduced **Brian May**, along with Neil Murray on bass. Tony Martin from Black Sabbath was there too, Darren Wharton, John Idan, Chris Thompson from Manfred Mann's Earthband who was fantastic, Bobby Rondinelli from Blue Oyster Cult. Black Sabbath and Rainbow and Pete French from Cactus and Atomic Rooster.

Throughout the concert Cozy's kit was on stage, lovingly protected by his drum roadie, who it is rumoured takes his remains in an urn on his motorbike every Sunday.

It was a very emotional evening, but I didn't have much time, to feel the sadness I had to prepare for the following nights Alexis Korner Concert

This year featured the wonderful **Eric Burdon** and he had invited **Aynsley Dunbar** to play drums for him. It was one of the finest sets I have ever been involved with. It was red hot from the first note.

Aynsley was magnificent of course so was John Price on bass and Tony Ashton on keyboards and I was absolutely having a ball. Eric really rocked that night.

Its ironic there is so much stuff on YouTube, and yet I have never been able to watch this set which is a pity.

It was really funny to watch Aynsley strip drums down from this enormous DW kit that had been supplied. He used a fraction of what they sent.

It was nice to bring in ex Rolling Stone Mick Taylor to Buxton at last too, wonderful guitarist *Chris Farlowe Paul Jones, Tom Robinson, Tony Ashton* gave the evening everything they had and *John Gorman & Mike McCartney* of the Scaffold compered the night with their own brand of mayhem.

Savoy Brown were always one of my favourite blues bands and never more so than when the inimitable Chris Youlden was with them.
So I was thrilled that he agreed to appear, and he did not disappoint, he has a rich idiosyncratic voice, and is a really great performer. I was having the time of my life up there.

In the October **Van Morrison** invited the band and Chris Farlowe to guest on his tour, always very generous to other artistes, contrary to what people imagine, many times Van has used some of his favourite singers and musicians as guests. We had no idea how long this tour would last, but it ran for about 8 years and even today we occasionally do them. We even got to play Van's 70th birthday party in Sept 2015.

The tour started in my hometown with two nights at the Manchester Apollo.
Van is a quiet guy and certainly does not seek publicity, and people look at this like he is uncooperative. But I have always found him a lot of fun, and we often have dinner together before the shows swapping stories mainly about old BBC Radio comedies like Al Read, Jimmy Clitheroe and Tony Hancock as we are both great fans.

This alongside our own projects and Chris Farlowe's European tours which took in Germany, Austria, Switzerland and Hungary, we were pretty hard at it.

1990 with Buddy Guy

1992 with Paul Jones

1995 with Jack Bruce (Buxton Opera House)

1995 with Jack Bruce and Dick Heckstall Smith
(Buxton Opera House)

1998 with Eric Burdon   (Buxton Opera House)

1998 album shoot

TWO THOUSAND

A new Chris Farlowe album seemed to come around very fast, I was back in the producer's chair this time in 2000. This was the album **"Glory Bound"** We recorded the backing tracks at a studio in Blackpool called Berlin owned by John Sykes of Thin Lizzy and Whitesnake.

The rest was recorded at Andy Scott's studio in beautiful Wiltshire. Andy of course famous for his guitar work with Sweet also engineered the sessions. The album was a mix of styles and even featured a string quartet on one track. It was a fun time making the album with various guests, Mick Green legendary guitarist with the Pirates, Paul Jones on harmonica, Chanter Sisters on backing vocals, Steve Simpson on Fiddle, Micky Moody on slide. and Brendan Gore on piano.

While we were recording some keyboard parts record label owner Kris Gray was dressed in denim shorts and his usual red Doc Martins and was taking a call whilst casually leaning against a rural gate, which was obviously not made for the purpose of leaning on. So, halfway through a piano take, we saw these red boots disappear down a hill through the now collapsed gate.

It looked so funny Dave Baldwin on keys had to stop playing through laughing.

We walked to the gate and found Kris in true businessman mode still talking on the phone like nothing had happened.

On the title track written by Mike D'abo, we had Steve Simpson on fiddle, and it created the effect I was looking for, a sort of haunting dirge. It was perfect first take, but I asked him to go in and do another, which again was perfect and when I put them together it was beautifully morose. It also featured Brendan Gore on piano

The Alexis show 2000 featured *Chris Farlowe, Paul Jones Mike Sanchez, Victor Brox Tony Ashton and Roy Harper,* who I had tried to get to the Concert several times, but he was always working.

We also did occasional gigs with Paul Jones, Jimmy Dawkins and Zoot Money.

Throughout 2001 we toured nearly all year with Chris Farlowe in Europe and when availability allowed with Van Morrison.

We also appeared at an open-air Festival in Eveleigh, Wiltshire with the legendary John Mayall. The weather was very unkind, it rained constantly but the crowd were in good spirits throughout. The stage was very slippery and wet, and the changeovers in equipment were quite perilous, and there was **John Mayall** then aged 67 carrying John Price's equipment through the wind and rain to our truck. John is truly an amazing man, very influential as was Alexis. In fact, it was Alexis that advised John that he would have to move to London to get recognition.

John was born near me in Macclesfield and was often found high in his tree house.

I also made an appearance on 'This is Your Life' the legendary TV show, it was the life of Paul Jones. I was in Koblenz with Chris Farlowe on tour, but they sent a camera team over, I felt very important. I never imagined Michael Aspel would say that was Norman Beaker it was very surreal.

It was turning into quite a year, while we were in Germany with Chris Farlowe, Van asked us if we would be available for three nights at the Royal Albert Hall.

In all the years I had been playing and having been lucky enough to play most named theatres including the Palladium and the like, I had never played The Albert Hall, and suddenly I was playing it three times.

It's an amazing venue, but Van always likes to be set up in a tight space, so it's a bit of a clubby atmosphere. So, the stage was vast but set up is tight. Chris Farlowe never one to hold back did mention it looked like his house "Filthy and full of strangers".

Later in the year we were invited to play a Festival in Moscow with Chris and the Yardbirds. The weather was minus twenty five degrees, I had never felt cold like it, thick snow everywhere but being daft Northern lads, having dropped our bags at the hotel, we decided to have a quick walk around the place.

Lenni looked at me startled when he saw my nose was pouring in blood, and within a couple of minutes several of us experienced the same thing. Apparently, it's so cold it dries the lining of the nasal passages and there you are, a bloody nose. But all was well after we had recovered, and we headed back to the hotel for a beer or two.

The hotel was keen to be paid in dollars or sterling which we were warned about, so we all had a few. So, at the bar with a fistful of dollars I buy John Price and myself a beer, and it was the equivalent of £12. John said it would be his round next.

I was interested to see how much it was going to cost in the restaurant which we were heading for. This time the beer was only about £6. Puzzled by this, I asked the barman why it was more expensive in the bar than the restaurant, and his reply was "this beer is piss". An honest man, it was too.

The whole experience was interesting; I was surprised how small Red Square was. When you see the military parades, I can only assume the tanks go around in circles.
So, the day of the gig arrives, we get in a car in which the heater was the only thing that worked properly. Halfway to the gig the driver said "I thought you were five", and we realised we had left the keyboard player at the hotel.

So, we go back to get him and finally we are on the way and looking forward to the gig, and to get in the warm too, until we discovered the venue was an ice rink. It's not all glamour we thought, but with a few expletives thrown in.

When it came to sound check time, I opened my guitar case to find the five-position switch on my Strat was now in the body where some kind luggage handler had decided to pile stuff on it.

Luckily and gratefully, Gypie Mayo who was playing in the Yardbirds after his stint with Dr Feelgood kindly lent me his Telecaster for the show. Gypie was a great player. He passed away in 2013 on October 23rd when he was 62 years old.

The gig was good and the audience too, though I felt sorry for them all rugged up standing on the ice.

The following morning, we were up early for the flight home, only to be told at the airport that the flight had been delayed by 3 hours. Just then Paul Burgess who was in the drum seat for this gig informed us that things had just got worse. When we enquired what could be worse he said "They are offering to feed us". Very funny, as we were not overly impressed with the cuisine.

On November 4th we held a memorial concert for Tony Ashton again at Buxton Opera House. We were starting to feel a bit like funeral chasers, but people kept asking us to organise them, and we enjoyed paying tribute to our friends and their musical associates. It was a lovely evening, and as I have already mentioned Tony was very dear to people, me included, I loved him to bits.

Good northern sense of humour. He once heard a couple of Scottish people talking in a pub, and joined in with a very convincing accent. They used to call him Scots Tony, little did he know it was Ewan McGregor and his Dad.

It was easy to get the musicians interested especially the Deep Purple guys, Jon Lord and Ian Paice were the first to say yes. Also *Zak Starkey, Geoff Whitehorn*, a favourite guitarist of mine, who I like very much, great sense of humour, *Henry Spinnetti, Dave Berry*, who although remembered for his hits such as the Crying Game, Little Things etc. was more known for his Blues and Rock stuff first, and always likes to play some blues when he can. *Colin Hodgkinson* on bass for some of it, *Neil Murray* was also on bass at times and guitarists *Miller Anderson, Micky Moody and Bernie Marsden, Gerraint Watkins* was on keyboards and any other instruments he could find. It was a really fitting tribute to Tony, a true character

Throughout 2002 we embarked on a 52 date tour of Europe with Chris Farlowe and many UK dates with Van made for a packed schedule. I was also doing the odd gig with Herbie Goins in Italy.

Of course, the Alexis Memorial had to be organised, and it was getting harder every year to find new artistes to the show, and I was so busy it was getting to be very stressful. But we managed to get through them and this year featured one of my favourite acoustic singer / songwriters Geoff Muldaur, great emotive yet clean vocalist. Geoff was married to Maria Muldaur who I really like also.

Also appearing were the legendary 9 Below Zero, Otis Grand, Mick Abrahams Todd Sharpville, Bob Hall and Victor Brox. It was a good night with a lot of controlled jamming which is always fun.

A single by Chris Farlowe and us **"I'll leave the Light on"** was released and even got us a spot on Top of the Pops 2. But they wanted a live version of "Out of Time" instead, That song is never far away since its release in 1966. It was quite a funny experience, all the young fans there watching us wondering what they were going to be subjected too, but not for long they were going crazy.

A guy came up and politely asked if he could watch us sound check and that his parents were fans. It was only when the programme was screened we realised it was Daniel Beddingfield who was number one that week, Mark Owen of Take That was on too, so a healthy Manchester contingent had invaded that London.

We recorded our third album with Kris Gray's Delicious label **"Who's He Calling Me Him"** the title which I should explain is about two men being noisy in a pub. The landlord asked them to keep the noise and bad language down. They ignored his request, and the landlord had enough, and says to the worst culprit, "Get out and take him with you". The other guy said, "who's he calling me him", and it just gave me an idea as an album title.

It was a lot of fun to make, and after the more melodic "The Older I get the Better I Was" album. This one went back more to the Blues roots, with the occasional melodic song. Chris Farlowe guested on the Tony Joe White song "The Guitar Don't Lie" a song that's been in Chris's set since our first tour with him, and a lot of people think I wrote it as they have heard me play it for so many years.

Micky Moody played slide on a couple of songs too. Sheila Gott again provided great backing vocals. The album got a lot of airplay.

In December we started recording Chris Farlowe's album **"Farlowe That"**. It was recorded at KDS Studios in Chiswick.

The year took in our usual tour schedule with Van and Chris Farlowe, and we also recorded quite a few albums.

In February we started work on a Miller Anderson album **"Bluesheart"** . Miller is a guitarist I've always respected a lot, and a great singer. The late Jon Lord played some organ on it too. Miller had worked with Jon a lot on various projects. We were also still finishing off the Chris Farlowe album "Farlowe That" and we started work on the **Cliff Bennett** album **"Nearly Retired"**. Always a fun time with Cliff, he is wonderful company.

In September we played the Hell Blues Festival in Norway. You can actually get your passport stamped to prove you have been to hell and back, It was a great night, my band with Chris

119

Farlowe, Miller Anderson, Bernie Marsden and Jon Lord on organ, for one night only we were known as the Hell Blues Band.

2004 brought a bit of a departure for us as we were booked to play as the House band on the "Hit Makers" tour. Originally the line up was to be Chris Farlowe, Cliff Bennett, Mike D'Abo and Dave Berry, all of which we had worked with before.

Unfortunately, Mike and Dave had been booked on another tour that contractually they had to fulfil. So, two replacements were sought at quite short notice, they were Dave Dee of Dozy, Beaky, Mick and Tich fame, and Chip Hawkes from the Tremoloes.

We had never met them before and certainly it was a very different genre for us. But after a few teething troubles on the opening night, I really enjoyed the musical change.

Every night the four singers swapped their order of appearance and so it stayed very fresh. I also enjoyed the comedy of Dave Dee and Cliff Bennett in particular.

Cliff had this act of looking like he was going to black out and lean on the microphone asking me if the nurse has shown up yet with the drugs etc. This he did every night, and it always made me helpless with laughter, so on one occasion I got him back. I bought a comedy nurses hat and apron which I wore under my jacket, and the hat behind my amp.

While Cliff was doing his patter, I pulled out the Apron donned the hat and the audience started to laugh and Cliff couldn't understand why until he turned to me, and almost collapsed laughing. He's a funny guy with a great sense of humour he had tears in his eyes, it was a really hilarious moment.

Dave Dee was also a funny guy, and a real professional, although one night playing his hit "Legend of Xanadu" he accidentally caught me with his bull whip that he used to crack intermittently, it hurt like hell I can tell you that much.

On the opening night, and out of the blue he asked me if I played mandolin and I said I had never tried "Well I fancy doing Bend It", which was one of Dave's big hits, so I ended up playing it on guitar with loads of chorus on it and it worked OK.

Dave unfortunately passed away in January 2009, he suffered with prostate cancer, but still performed right to the end. He was 67.

I really enjoyed performing some of the Tremeloes hits with Chip Hawkes adding a bit of a new blues dimension. Chip's a very fine musician and a lovely guy. All in all, I had a great time on the tour.

Earlier in the year we did a gig in Emmen, Holland with Chris Farlowe, at the Giraffe Club and the Troggs were also on the bill. I really enjoyed the gig, and I told the Troggs guitarist the same thing, I also told him I preferred his playing to the original guitarist Chris Britton, I nearly died when he said, "I am Chris Britton", I had to try and cover myself by telling him I was only joking that I knew all along, I'm not sure he bought it though.

On the 21st June 2004 which just happened to be my birthday a tribute concert to Lonnie Donegan was held at the Royal Albert Hall. I was asked to participate with Chris Farlowe to play "Alabamy Bound". It was a wonderful evening, and everyone played a song from Lonnie's back catalogue.

It was nice to see so many stars there including Mark Knopfler, Van Morisson, Joe Cocker, Billy Bragg, Roger Daltrey, Bruce Welch, Chas and Dave, Chris Barber, Arlo Guthrie, Ralph McTell, Joe Brown, Barron Knights, Gerry Marsden and many more from all spheres of entertainment. It was a fitting tribute to a wonderful man.

I very much enjoyed chatting with Bruce Welch he was really interesting, and he even showed me a few Shadows dance steps.

As well as the Hit Makers tour, we did a tour of Sweden which was a bit of a disaster due to an incompetent promoter. This was followed with a 40 date tour of Germany, Austria, Belgium and Poland with Chris Farlowe.

John Price had to leave the tour due to other commitments at the start of the Polish leg of the tour. A really fine bass player called Russell Milton stood in as he had done, for the Hit Makers tour.

He was a real laugh, but in a nice way a bit of a loose cannon, and things often went wrong for him, not always his fault, just bad luck and circumstances.

His first night started when he arrived before us at the Radisson hotel in Szczecin. He attempted to check in but his name wasn't on the list. It was down as John Price, my name was under Norman Hume, Chris Farlowe was under Deighton and so on.
We found him looking very forlorn in the foyer and I told him he could share my room. It was like a huge suite so it was no problem.

So far so good, we both go to sleep, but a few hours later there comes a loud knock on the door. I got up opened it and there were two gigantic burly guys holding the arms of this naked bass player, and I mean naked. He stood there looking more than a little sheepish.

Apparently he had sleepwalked into the lift and had been spotted by security on CCTV, so as he got out of the lift to go to reception, the security men just turned him round and brought him to my room.

One of the heavies asked me if I knew this guy, and for a moment I thought should I say no just for a joke, but judging by the face of these guys I decided against it.

Throughout 2005/ 6 / 7 / we toured extensively with Chris Farlowe all over Europe, which culminated with an appearance on the legendary German WDR TV show Rockpalast, which is still being shown occasionally to this day, and is on general release on both CD and DVD.

In 2005 we released a live album with Chris recorded at the Gastroblues Festival in 2004 in Paks in Hungary with bonus tracks from a gig at Charleys in Oldenburg, The album appropriately enough entitled **"Hungary For The Blues"**

We also did the a lot of guest spots on the never ending Van Morrison tours culminating in an another appearance at the Royal Albert Hall in 2007, and including a lot of Festivals. One in particular springs to mind in the Autumn of 2006 , at the Battle Festival in Sussex.

The weather had been bad and Van was coming by helicopter to the gig. We heard a lot of commotion from the crew who had discovered the chopper had landed in the wrong field, and so they sent a quad bike to bring him, the indignity of it all.

In 2008 we did a session on the Paul Jones show with the legendary soul blues singer **Herbie Goins,** a real character and great company. We just did a few gigs to test the water with him as he had not been to England since the first Alexis Korner Memorial gig in 1994. I had done a few festivals with him in Italy but that was all.

He had very bad hearing problem since his days in the army where he was a tank trainer, and as he once told me "The first thing you teach is don't touch nothing until I tell you". Apparently these instructions were not heeded and two of the big guns went off right next to him and shattered his ear drums, and on top of that just to compound the situation, on his arrival at the hospital the doctors decided he had to have all his wisdom teeth out as well.

Obviously it was a bit of a problem rehearsing as Herbie refused to wear his hearing aid. So when we ran through some new stuff on acoustic instruments he couldn't tell where he should come in and used to stare blankly at us.

We also did a very memorable concert with Chris Farlowe and the wonderful **Madeline Bell**, two of the great vocalists on one night at the Princess Theatre Torquay. It was nice to meet the legendary Dionne Warwick that evening too who was a big friend of Madeline's. She was great fun, really down to earth woman.

In April 2009 we began a 30 date tour called "Souled on Blues", and it featured Cliff Bennett, Herbie Goins and the ubiquitous Chris Farlowe. Added to this was a huge European tour with Chris, these tours were getting longer and longer.

The Soul'd on Blues tour was a lot of fun, Herbie stayed with me for about two months, and spent hours reading an atlas of Europe. He was a big hit in my local pub The Moor Top in Heaton Moor, Stockport. He was a true gentleman much appreciated by everyone.

He was a big Church goer and had a case full of clothes for every occasion, even one for the Church. On one occasion I asked him if the sermon was good, he said "I don't know, I couldn't hear, but it looked good".

He was always losing stuff too, wallets, jackets, money anything we had to take good care of him, but he was lovely and a great voice.

He once asked me if anyone else in my family had been in music, and remembering a joke my Father told me, I told him. "My Uncle was on the stage, and he fell through it, if he hadn't have had a rope around his neck he could have hurt himself",, he thought it was so hilarious he made me retell the story to everyone he met.

He also loved Weatherspoons pubs too. He couldn't believe how cheap it was and would tell anyone who would listen.

We played the Keitele Jazz Festival in Eidsvoll in Finland on July 22nd, also on the bill a good friend of ours **Spencer Davis** who sadly passed away 19th October 2020, and the Animals. It was an amazing Festival. On keyboards for the Animals was

Mickey Gallagher a great player known for his work with the Blockheads and the Clash. And we were so proud when Mickey asked to hang around with us, because it looked like fun and it was too. Finland at that time of the year had daylight long into the night. It was a lovely setting for a Festival, and we were taken for a cruise around the islands. We had a great time

Top of the bill that night was Procul Harum with the late and very great Gary Brooker who passed away 19th February 2022, aged 76, and guitar wizard Geoff Whitehorn. We were all travelling on the same coach, and having a few drams of Bushmills whiskey, feeling in good spirits. We proceeded to sing classic Procol songs in a pub singers style, Gary did a fine northern rendition of Whiter Shade of Pale. However, for Gary the fun was short lived.

As we pulled up for a toilet break Gary wandered off and climbed a log pile which collapsed under him, and he cracked several ribs. He was taken to hospital and was bandaged up around his chest. He tried his best to perform, but it was not possible for him to complete the show. I ended up playing with Spencer and the Animals to fill some of the show time, I loved it.

And Geoff Whitehorn did some Procol Vocals, good rhyme there.

On the subject of Spencer, I received news of his demise, all be it prematurely, I knew he had been ill for a long time, so it wasn't unexpected, but the info was wrong. By the time I found out my error, I had written a bit of a eulogy on Facebook to let his fans know. Soon after Zoot Money phoned to tell me that it was wrong oops.

I later got a few emails from Spencer saying things like "It's nice here on the other side" and "not many gigs up here". Nice to see he took it so well. Sadly, when Spencer did pass away, I decided I wouldn't write anything just in case. He was a kind and modest man, sadly missed.

Many years had passed since I had last seen Larry Garner, one of the greatest of modern Blues men in my opinion, great storyteller, great voice, great writer, and a hot guitar player.

We actually met again via Facebook, a positive internet story. We had a good messaging session, and I asked if he had any plans to come to the UK. He told me he would love to come over, so I told him I would look into it and put the word around a few agents.

We got enough offers to make it viable and decided on Oct 8th we would record a live album at the Tivoli Theatre in Wimborne, which is run by a good friend Charlie North Lewis. The recording and the gig were both really good, and we had a great brass section of Kim Nishikawara on saxes and flute, and Steve "Howey" Hallworth on trumpet and Flugelhorn. The album was going to be put out to coincide with a tour planned for the following year.

We also did a session for the Paul Jones show, recorded at Maida Vale, and the following night we played in Paris at the Sunset Sunside. It started in panic after the Maida Vale session, we were leaving the car at a friends and I couldn't find my passport. I was really panicking, to say the least. Autumn leaves everywhere, torrential rain, a needle in a haystack had never been more apt.

And Larry said, "what's that shit under the back wheel", and there it was, Oh thank you Gods.

We had a great night in Paris just Larry, John Price, Steve Gibson on drums and myself.

2008 with Chris Farlowe

Finland 2009 with Spencer Davis in Finland

2009 Larry Garner Tivoli Wimborne

2009 With John Price in Paris

With Chris Barber at the Royal Albert Hall 2007

TWO THOUSAND AND TENS

2010 We toured with Larry extensively in the UK, Spain and Germany, to promote the album **"Live at the Tivoli"**. It was very successful and a lot of great times followed. Larry and myself have always had a great relationship, and enjoy each other's company a lot. He makes me laugh so much. We did a great gig in Spain at the Bejar Jazz and Blues Festival. On the bill were the Fabulous Thunderbirds, Canned Heat and old friends of ours Climax Blues Band.

The venue was a bull ring, said to be the oldest one in Spain. We arrived at the venue, which unfortunately was more than Larry's luggage had, it had gone to another country altogether. So, he ended up playing in T Shirt and jeans, but Larry always can carry clothes off unlike me. The gig was great, but as the late Larry the ("Mole") Taylor, bassist with Canned Heat, went on stage, his bass malfunctioned for some reason so he borrowed John Price's for his set.

We also managed to cram quite a few dates with Chris Farlowe in too, we finished the year off with him at the legendary 100 Club.

2011 we continued touring with Larry and Chris Farlowe, as we have for many years by now, but myself and John Price were now also performing as a duo, We did a few gigs in Holland and Luxembourg, it was a nice change.

We also worked with Cliff Bennett at a few gigs, always a pleasure, but unpredictable. We played the Pavillion in Margate, it was like a blast from the old ballroom gig days. It all went according to plan, when at the end Cliff left the stage to an ovation. We had planned to do Robert Parkers "Barefootin", so we did the big intro, and I was doing the 'big welcome back to the stage routine'. We just kept playing round the brass intro, again and again then again, still no Cliff, so I sang it myself. We went into the dressing room later. I asked Cliff what happened, he said "I was a bit tired," and that was that. And that is typical Cliff, very laid back.

In July we performed at the legendary San Javier Jazz & Blues Festival and it was one of the hottest places I have ever played. The soundcheck in the middle of the day was dangerously hot, I couldn't even touch the guitar strings the heat was so great. It was one of the only times I thought the heat would kill me. Even when we were on stage at around 9pm it was still scorching.

In August I did a couple of gigs with Jack Bruce and my band, the first which was broadcast on the BBC and was recorded at the Colne International R & B Festival. Jack was quite fragile health wise, but he was still playing like a demon. The following day we played the Rhythm Festival in Biggleswade in Bedfordshire, and it was raining like crazy, and then as if by magic, as Jack played the opening riff to "Sunshine of your love", an amazing rainbow arched above the stage, It was quite something. It was so nice to be playing with Jack again after his long illness.

These dates were followed by a couple of dates with Maggie Bell and Chris Farlowe.

And we ended the year with a long German tour throughout November and December

In 2010 we topped the bill at the Monaghan Harvest Festival with Larry which was great, but I felt we were missing out on some of the atmosphere. So, I asked the organiser if we could come back and play the Blues route, next year. You have to play three gigs at a different venue every day.

He agreed, but also said that it was the first time any band had requested that after headlining.

We enjoyed the experience very much, met loads of people and felt part of the whole Festival.

We were not sure originally if we had made the right decision when the first gig was up loads of stairs on a fire escape and it was pouring with rain to make it worse. But that apart the night was great.

The following day we were listening to a lot of the other acts such as Otis Taylor, but one I really wanted to see was Steve James, I had loads of CDs of his, but I had never seen him. So we went to the gig which had already started, and he played lots of stuff in a way I'd never heard him do, but was really entertaining.

So, after the show I told him I was a fan, so he and my band and myself went for a coffee together. He was more radical than I had imagined. We had a couple of beers and some good chat. When it was time to go to our next gig he walked part of the way with us, where we saw a poster of him, but it had the wrong picture on it. He said no that's fine. It turned out we had been enjoying the company of Watermellon Slim. We saw the wrong gig and got drunk together with the wrong man. One of the band didn't miss the opportunity to say "I thought you were supposed to know about Blues"
I have to say though Slim was fascinating to chat with, so it worked out great.

At the final gig on the Sunday night, there was to be a big closing show at the Marquee we had played at the previous year. The landlord of the pub said, while we were packing up, that he was going over to the Marquee, "here are the keys lock up when you go." Now that is trust, a Blues band left alone in a pub. But we behaved impeccably. It had been a great weekend, just like the old days.

2012 was busy, the whole year was filled with European and UK dates and with Chris Farlowe and Larry Garner, and a September European tour for my band.

In June we did a few gigs with **Dave Berry**, one which just happened to be my Birthday June 21st. Dave announced it to the audience at the Tivoli Theatre in Wimborne.

So after a rousing rendition of Happy Birthday to you, he informed the audience, " I'm not going to tell you how old Norman is, but you are looking at two hundred pounds worth of heating allowance". Really lovely guy and a great sense of humour. He had a big influence on many artistes with his menacing use of the microphone. He's a real music aficionado especially in the Blues and Rock and Roll genres.

On the same birthday gig, he also informed the crowd about our drinking prowess, untrue of course but quite funny. He said "I've only been with Norman and the guys for a few days, but they can drink for England, so last night I told them that I would be having an early night, no alcohol. So, in my room I started to read this magazine that had an article on excess drinking and liver failure etc, and it changed my life forever. I informed Norman that when we we're touring together in future, I will never read again". Always a great, night with Dave.

We had been trying to record a new album in our own right, but we had been touring and recording so much, hadn't had time to do it. 2013 This was to be put right with a duo album from John Price and myself which we recorded at Johns studio, over a much longer period of time than we had expected due to other commitments. But we got there in the end. The album was called **"Between the Lines"**, and it presented a mix of my originals and some standard Blues and reworkings of some popular songs. The song that started it all for me was the Buddy Holly hit "It doesn't matter anymore". It was my talent contest winning song and my Mums favourite so I decided to record it as a very slow Gospel arrangement in memory of her.

We also released **"A Good Night in Vienna"**, a live album with Larry Garner, which was a little more raw than the previous Tivoli album. No brass players on this, much more guitar based.

Audiences seem to really like the juxtaposition of Larry's really authentic American style, and my very British one.

It seems to cover all bases and adds a bit of charm, and they always love the humour, and of course Larry's story telling is worth the admission price alone.

We toured extensively with him to promote the album in Europe.

On Saturday May 17th we played a wonderful gig with Jack to celebrate his 70th Birthday, a Blues cruise from Helsinki to Stockholm. The plane to Helsinki was late, but the crew managed to hold up the boat for 1 hour until we arrived, which Jack really enjoyed. Wee felt very privileged, it was a lot of fun. Jack was on great form, we chatted and laughed late into the night.

Unfortunately, this would be the last gig I would ever play with him, so it was a fitting finale and one of so many great memories of playing together. He truly was an inspiration to me, and we were very close, it's doubly hard to lose someone who is a great friend, and a genius of a musician to work alongside.

But I was very fortunate to have spent so much time on and off stage with him. a very special man.

2013 was also our first tour of the Balkans, under the close scrutiny of the agent and tour manager **Nebojsa Petrovic** boss of the RockSvirke agency. He used to be a Serbian basketball coach, needless to say he is huge, in build and personality.

It was great to see the region first hand. We had some preconceptions, but we were very wrong, especially about the food.

It was very interesting to observe their diet. They eat huge meals, but there are very few obese people, and they seem to eat more protein than carbs.

The audiences were amazingly responsive and were so pleased we went there to play for them. It was a great experience, and they certainly know how to promote, and the media is very interested, I did so many TV Radio and press interviews.

Many times, we would pull into a service station to do an interview on the way to a gig. Sometimes the accommodation was not what we are used to, but it's a good reality check.

We did a couple of nights in June with Chris Farlowe and Van Morisson at the very picturesque Dunluce Castle in Bushmills, a beautiful place set in County Antrim, Northern Ireland overlooking the sea. It was amazing to be playing there as the sun went down behind the horizon.

Some nights are such a magical experience and make me realise how lucky I have been doing this for a living. Van's daughter Shana was also on the gig. She has a great voice and I really liked her album 7 Wishes.

In October we did a rare tour of France with Larry, and I have to admit the sound engineers at all venues were amazing, They really know there onions, no pun intended, and the venues were great too.

One of the venues we played was the very well established Jazz / Blues Club Le Duc des Lombards in Paris. We played two shows there in one night, one at 8pm then that audience departed, then at 10pm the next house came in and we did it all over again.

It was a lovely venue, and a great gig but with one exception, getting there with your backline.

We were told it's not possible to park the near the venue, so drive to the gig unload and we will tell you where to park, They said drive here, (showing us a map) park and get the train back. Yes that's how far away it was.

We did this but if there is ever a need for in house backline, this has to be it.

We did a lot of gigging in 2014 with more French dates one of which was Disneyland in Paris with Larry Garner. It was very strange affair with in ear monitoring and amps miles away and no audience response to be heard. It was quite difficult as Larry likes to work an audience, a very macabre experience.

It was another year of intensive touring. We again toured the Balkans but this time as a trio. It made economic sense, and it gave us a chance to stretch ourselves away from the safety of a five piece. The three of us John Price bass, Steve Gibson drums and myself really enjoyed the more edgy hard hitting down home blues of yesteryear.

We took in gigs in Slovakia, Croatia and Serbia, and really enjoyed ourselves meeting the fans. It's a love of mine checking out the various customs across Europe

We did a European tour with Larry Garner April and May, then a few dates with Chris Farlowe in June. It was starting to get as one tour finished as the next started.

July came and we were back in Serbia and Croatia with the whole band.

We decided to take the whole of August off, as we really were running on empty. Of course, I was still writing songs and planning for the coming years so you never totally switch off.

Unfortunately, on October 25th I got the news I had been expecting that Jack Bruce had passed away. It hit me much harder than I had expected. From that day every gig I have played I have featured a Jack tribute song.

His funeral was on November 5th. It was a very moving ceremony held at Golders Green Crematorium in London. It was a very private ceremony with invited friends. Ginger Baker and Eric Clapton were both there obviously, Gary Brooker, Phil Manzanera from Roxy Music, Uli Jon Roth, and Kip Hanrahan who Jack worked a lot with. There was a lovely poignant moment when Pete Brown long time friend and lyricist, read a poem he had written specially for the ceremony.
And the ceremony finished with the congregation all singing Strawberry Fields for ever.
The end of an era, and so many great memories.

In March 2015 we embarked on our first major Trio tour of Slovakia, Slovenia, Croatia and Serbia which resulted in us recording the gig in Belgrade at the Dom Omladine on the 27th March. The cryptically entitled album **"Live in Belgrade"** was released later in the year.

We did think of calling it 'Never mind the Balkans' but didn't want to start a diplomatic incident.

We invited Rebecca Downes to guest with us on some of the gigs. She's a fine singer and was good fun to have around, very low maintenance.

One downside was when we got in the car on the way to the gig, she managed to trap my hand in the door, which was fully closed, but apart from the pain there was no damage, God really smiled on me that night. But she was so apologetic, and never stopped saying how's your hand, every ten minutes.

It was getting quite difficult to fit all the touring in as we had a Larry Garner European tour in May and part of June, some of our gigs promoting the trio album and also a tour of Germany, Austria and Slovakia with Chris Farlowe in the September.

In the November a good friend of ours Michael Ford who used to promote the Bronte Blues Club gigs in Keighley, Yorkshire, was organising the first P & O Blues Cruise from Hull to Rotterdam and back. It was so much fun we played our own set and with Kyla Brox, who has a great voice like her Father Victor and Mother Annette.

It was quite odd as I had known Kyla from being a baby and I made possibly the worst introduction on stage. I said, "Ladies and Gentlemen here is someone I have known even before she was born Mr Kyla Brox", thankfully Kyla as always saw the funny side. She is such good fun. We finished the year with some Christmas concerts with Chris Farlowe.

2016 was just as busy as ever starting with a Larry Garner European tour in February and March, quickly followed by a Trio tour of Poland in the April and May. The Trio was meant just to be a filler in between Beaker band tours. It was nice to play a little more rocky improvised stuff, but it really took off with the release of the "Live in Belgrade" album. The Polish tour

137

was really interesting and so were the venues, I hadn't been back to Poland since the Chris Farlowe tour in 2004. Due to E.U money, the roads and infrastructure had massively improved. The audiences were very knowledgeable and appreciative, it was a great experience and the Trio had some great plays.

In August /September we did our usual Annual European tour with Chris Farlowe, and once again did the P & O Blues Cruise this year with Larry Garner and Kyla again.
It was a never to be forgotten trip. There was a force 10 gale and the ship was really rocking, On stage the curtains were swinging out into the audience and the amps were rolling from side to side behind us, it was really rough.
Larry looked like he was going to fall backwards into the drums and trying to play a wah wah pedal on one leg took a great deal of concentration and balance.

We continued with a Larry Garner tour of Germany and Sweden which was a nice change for us, and the gigs were wonderful. As always a tour with Larry is always special and a lot of laughs.

Being a huge football fan the 50th anniversary of England's World Cup victory was a sad reminder of our decline. But Chris Farlowe was in great demand as I previously mentioned. He was number one in the Charts or Hit Parade as it was then with **"Out of Time"** so everyone wanted him at the same time. It was nice.I got to meet a few famous footballers through these shows. Including George Cohen the World Cup winning right back.

2011 with Herbie Goins (photo Alan White)

2013 (photo Paul Wolfgang Webster)

2013 Norman (photo Ian Corbridge)

2014 with Chris Farlowe

2016 Shepherds Bush Empire   "Night for Jack "
(photo Arnie Goodman)

2018 with Steve Ellis

(photo Paul Wolfgan Webster)

Norman Beaker Trio
L to R John Price, Leo Andjelkovic and me in Croatia

BLUES HALL OF FAME

On the 18th January 2017 the biggest surprise of my life came to pass. I had been inducted into the **Blues Hall of Fame** as a legendary British Blues artist one of only 9 in the 20th century, Eric Clapton, Mick Jagger, Keith Richard, John Mayall, Peter Green, Jack Bruce, Gary Moore, Jeff Beck and me. I have joked ever since I'm the only one I hadn't heard of.

Initially I thought it was a wind up, so I kept it to myself until our tour co-ordinator Sally Jane Sharp-Paulsen, confirmed it to me by email. It was a very strange feeling for me, I have won awards before but not on a this scale. Sally had helped bring me to the attention of the American Heritage International Organisation, of which I had no idea about, and for my services to blues I was inducted. Though I have never thought much about awards, this meant a lot to me, due to the company I was in, massive names like John Lee Hooker, Buddy Guy, Muddy Waters etc. It seemed surreal that a Manchester lad was included in this elite company.

Even Mike Sweeney legendary BBC Radio Manchester DJ remarked in an interview "So how did a Manchester scruff feel about this awar?" haka typical Sweeney a very good friend of mine so he was allowed to make this comment.

We did two shows in Stockport at our favourite local gig the Spinning Top, as a thank you to everyone for their support and it was sold out in days. It was a very special time, and I felt very humbled by the whole thing. Even now when people mention it to me I get really shy, which is unlike me, a bit like a kid being patted on the head from his parents for a good exam result.

But I'm so grateful for everyone's good wishes especially the musical fraternity.

Also, to commemorate the award we decided to record a new studio album the first for a few years.

We had recorded two live albums with Larry and a duo one with John Price and myself but not a band project.

So, it was a good time to record with the current band line-up with John Price on bass as for the last decades, Steve Gibson on drums, Nick Steed on keys Kim Nishikawara on saxes, and section stuff with Steve "Howie" Hallworth on trumpet.

The great soul & blues singer **Steve Ellis** famed for his massive hit "**Everlasting Love**" with Love Affair guested on the ballad "Time & Tide", and did a great job full of emotion, and Larry Garner contributed guitar and vocals to the track "I don't want a lover".

We recorded it at Strange Reality Studios in Snaith in Yorkshire a really nice studio to work in. The studio is owned by Chris Miley who has worked as our sound engineer on tours and gigs, so he knew instinctively what we were looking for.

I had written the sixteen tracks over a number of years, and had revisited and updated some, and I wrote one more or less in the studio. We were determined to make it as live as possible, and I think we succeeded.
The album title "**We See Us Later**" is the German translation for I'll see you later.

We got legendary photographer **Paul Wolfgang Webster** to take the cover pictures. I started to record the vocal tracks, and they were going so well, I didn't want to stop until I had sung all 15 tracks including backing vocals, in case the day after my voice might be shot to pieces. We went straight to the pub after that session.

We also played the Windsor festival again this time with the wonderful Sonja Kristina of Curved Air. She was every young man's dream girl at the time, and a very talented singer and performer. It was quite a departure for us, prog rock but it was nice to be out of our comfort zone. We also played on the same gig with Pete Brown .

In February 2018 we embarked on a Norman Beaker Band tour of Hungary / Romania / Serbia /Bulgaria / Slovenia and Croatia. The audiences grow all the time and appear to be very knowledgeable of most genres. We were going to be busy most of the year promoting the "We See Us Later" album which turned out to be very popular.

We then toured with Larry Garner in April in Germany and Holland so we were certainly cramming a lot of gigs in, but it's something I love still.

In September we played the fantastic Rockuja Festival in Poland, It's such a beautiful setting, a permanent site that has been built into a huge crater and illuminated caves surrounding the 20,000 seater venue.

We had an early flight followed by a 2 hour drive, then straight to the sound check. We were all a bit tired but as usual, the adrenaline takes over and the set with Chris Farlowe was fantastic.

Also on the bill were Ten Years After, good friends of ours, with Colin Hodgkinson on bass, the original drummer Ric Lee and Marcus Bonfanti vocals and guitar. It goes without saying the after party drinks were flowing, and a lot of catching up and laughs.

We also performed the Secret Widget Festival at Hurtswood Park Polo Club owned by Small Faces drummer Kenny Jones, very nice guy, wonderful setting, and some great bands on, Focus, Martin Barre, and a band that were on before us on the other stage from the Isle of Wight called LUCID. Unbelievable talents, all the members have great voices but the two twin girls Blue and Sunny Brown have such an angelic quality, I was almost late to do our set as I watched their set to the end.

2019 started very sadly as my first wife Carol passed away. She had been ill for a long time but still makes you think of happier times, I was surprised how upset I was at the funeral as we had not seen much of each other since 1986, but I think being the mother of Alex made it twice as bad.

In January and February we toured with the new look Trio John Price on bass, myself and multi instrumentalist and producer Leo Andjelkovic on drums from Novi Grad, but now living in Zagreb.

We met him when he came to one of our trio gigs in Croatia, and we were really impressed with his enthusiasm. for all aspects of the music business, although he was slightly worse for wear.

Leo knows how to enjoy himself. It was really refreshing, and gave us a new lease of life, not that we needed it. But it really helps to play with different people, sometimes you learn a lot from an occasional change of personnel.

The tour was a really big success, of course. It had been put together meticulously by **Nebojsa Petrovic** and his company **Rock Svirke** who work so hard in difficult circumstances, but is always on hand to help, and even drives the trio and looks after us so well.

The tour took in Croatia, Slovenia, Bosnia, Serbia, Romania, Bulgaria and for the first time in many years Greece. It was a great surprise to see how popular we were there and how fanatical the audiences are particularly on Jazz and Blues. All the gigs were sold out and we made many good friends there.

It was a nice moment when we were just leaving the venue to go and eat, and we had to go through the queue, and I heard this woman say in an English accent "There he is". It materialised that the lady had bought her daughter a ticket to see us as a birthday present, and she was so thrilled. So, we made a big fuss of her and left her a t-shirt and plectrum etc. It's so nice to share these moments.

Shortly after our return from the tour on 27th February, my bass player and long-time friend John Price was diagnosed to have a sarcoma, and would need an operation to remove it, and chemotherapy afterwards. John and myself have always believed in living your life and being grateful for what we have.

This certainly brought mortality sharply into focus. John has always been a fit guy, so it came as a big shock. He had the operation in May and luckily for all concerned it went well but now is a process of recovery. As John had to wait for the op and treatment, we were lucky enough to get Russell Milton back on bass, now a much changed character, but as always a lot of fun and great player. He fitted in really well, however this tour was going to be quite an ordeal.

A month before the tour was going to commence, Larry told me he was feeling unwell and might not be able to do it. After a series of hospital tests however he was given the go ahead, so as I was the only one knew about both Larry and John's illnesses, I felt like I had the whole thing on my shoulders. But it was now all going to happen which was a great relief as I had not told the booker or any promoters, and it was getting late in the day to cancel.

So, we were waiting for Larry to arrive but no such luck, his flight was cancelled until the following day, and the same thing happened the day after. Luckily, we had booked the tickets with a 2 day gap before we had to leave for the continent, so we had to change plans as he was now flying into London instead of Manchester. We arranged to pick him up there and take the Eurotunnel. Of course, it could and did get worse, his luggage had not arrived, it had gone to Manchester. So, we had to arrange to have it sent to Germany for us to pick up the following day.

But we were here at least in Europe and now ready for the tour, which I was happy to see was coming to fruition.

But things were about to take another turn when after a gig in Baden Baden the tour manager was taken ill and we had to send for an ambulance. He was rushed to hospital with sepsis and was really ill. Fortunately, he has made a full recovery.

So, the March / April tour, came to a good conclusion, it had been against all the odds and John Price's treatment was going well, although not yet match fit.

We did a nice few gigs with my old mate Zoot Money, very talented guy and great company. We did a gig at the Cheese and Grain in Frome, and the legendary Geno Washington was on the bill also, another real character so it was great listening to some of the anecdotes.

We had a band tour of Holland, Belgium and Germany in Sept for which John Sandham would take over on bass. Like Russell before him he did a wonderful job and was good company too. The tour was really enjoyable.

Later in September John Price was back and raring to go after a long steady recovery, and we decided the time was right to get back to our trio format. So with Leo Andjelkovic on drums we toured Poland, Slovenia and Croatia. It was a massive success, so much so we started to plan recording a studio album in 2020. Besides being a great drummer Leo is a great sound engineer and producer so we knew we would have a good team.

So, with our annual Christmas gigs in Stockport at the Spinning Top, and one in Newcastle with Chris Farlowe, a very eventful year had come to a successful conclusion, and we were very optimistic about the coming year.

TWO THOUSAND AND TWENTIES

Few could have foreseen what was to occur in 2020

January started in a very exciting and fun way, as we set about recording our new album **"Running Down The Clock"**. We recorded it at Sound Station Studio in Zagreb, Croatia.

I had written all the songs, always keeping in mind that we could reproduce them live, and they were all brought perfectly to life without any problems. We arrived at the studio the night before we were due to start recording just to set up and were contemplating going for a beer, but in the end, we recorded 4 tracks. It was a very organic process. It's very rare indeed when everything gels so easily.

We recorded a further fourteen songs, and we put them all on the album.

We co-produced it, and Leo and Mauro Sirol mastered it, and did a great job and it really did keep the live feel we were trying to achieve. As the album coincided with my 50 years in the "business" I decided to write songs that touched on all styles that have influenced me, so there are a lot of different genres, but all played with a big blues influence.

It was a very happy experience. We stayed at Leo's house with his family, being well fed by Leo's partner Milka. I named her the The Queen of soups. Boris Hrepic Hrepa guested on harmonica, and his wife Rola on backing vocals along with James Perri.

We were really excited with the outcome of this album, and really looking forward to touring and promoting it, and managed to do a little taster tour in early March to try out the new material.

We had a gig in Bergamo which had been cancelled due to the killer Covid 19, which none of us knew much about. It was worrying but not all consuming, so we played gigs in Croatia, Slovenia, Austria and France. We were just told to keep our hands sanitized, which we did. but we were being fairly ambivalent to what was going on. but not for long.

The last gig of this mini tour was in Nevers in France and on the way, there were overhead signs on the motorways, warnings about Corona virus.
In retrospect, it was very dangerous, the gig was packed. People were getting up real close, grabbing us in a friendly way I mean, but we were very concerned when we returned home.

We had a gig in Darlington at the Forum and on Friday 13th March there was a big change in protocol. No hand shaking and lots social distancing taking place, it was very surreal to us all.

Luckily the gig was great, and we had a great night, as did the audience. It was almost as if we all knew that this would be the last one for a while.

The official lock down date was announced by Health minister Matt Hancock on the 16th March but it was not until 20th March that pubs and clubs etc. were told to close. We, like many, had all our gigs and tours cancelled up a tentative restart in September.

We decided to release the album digitally in June. to give our fans the chance to hear the stuff, even if they couldn't see us live. It seemed to work as it got to number 2 in the iTunes Blues chart. The CD finally came on August 1st.
We had to reschedule about 80 gigs but the people's health had to come first. We at least had the album to promote which was lucky for us as many other bands were locked out of the studios. So, I did a lot of radio promotion, by telephone of course, and our distributors Anthony Broza, Laura Berman and Patrick Swift of Wienerworld organised a lot of great promotion.
2021, was always going to be different for everyone due to the pandemic, and the lockdowns were very strict. So, it was July before the rescheduled gigs were coming in. It was the longest

time I had ever had away from gigging, and although frustrating we were all in the same situation, so we just got on with it.

Personally, the televised football even without crowds kept me going. I don't usually get time to see that much. I was slightly concerned about my stamina level and how it would stand up to a long and very intense tour, but I was pleasantly surprised. I had bags of energy, even more than normal, so I can only assume it was due to the break that my body recharged itself. Whatever caused it I was so happy to be back playing. The audiences were all wonderful, I think it was everyone waking up to the reality of how important music is to everyone, musicians and public alike.

We started the tour at the Split Blues Festival in Croatia on the 24th July and it ran until 28th November which took in 17 countries.

John had to miss some of the tour as he had to be available for his treatment. So, his place was taken by Boris Hrepic from Dalmatia. He did a great job and fitted in perfectly musically and personally. We will be recording a new trio album this year if everything works out.

EPILOGUE

As Larry Garner has often said after one of his stories "That's all I've got to say about that".

I hope you've enjoyed joining me rambling through my memories, not always easy chronologically, well not with my memory anyway. It shows what you can do with a bit of talent and more importantly a hell of a lot of determination and tenacity. There are many things I still want to do, retirement is not an option for me, unless health dictates it. The excitement is the same for me as the first gig I ever did. The buzz of playing is very addictive, and blues in particular is great for keeping your emotions on red alert. It's very cathartic. Many people have wondered if not being as famous as some of my contemporaries bothers me at all, I can honestly say, hand on heart, no. All I ever wanted to do was to play the music I love and getting paid for it allowed me to continue doing it. The legendary musicians I have worked with and been good friends with are beyond price, I have gained so much life experience of many different cultures that I doubt I could have discovered in any other job.

Finally, I would like to thank the musicians, that have all enhanced my life in some way, promoters, fans, family and friends, for giving me such a great life and so many memorable times, I've been a very fortunate guy.

Credits
Monika Leupold, Gunter Leuers, Fritz Lang, John Holmes, Damian Hand, Dave Lewis, Neil Shaw Hulme, Paul Bamford, Sally Jane Sharpe-Paulsen, Mike Swan, JHS, Vintage Guitars, Derek Quinn, Lindsay Reade, Wienerworld, Anthony Broza, Laura Berman, Patrick Swift, John Mangan, Ian Brookes, Tony Whalley, Tony Kelly, Tony Nichols, Bob Oates, Mike Pickford, Derek Nash, Howard Coppitch, Andy Burns, Josh, Angeline Peeters, Theo and Diana, Tony Chapell, Jane Fraser, Eddy Bonte, Lut, Harry Shapiro, Steve Delaney, Dave Plimmer, and Beryl Hankin. Clive Mellor.

DISCOGRAPHY CREDITS

1971	**MORNING AFTER**	Blue Blood	Sky
1981	**NO MYSTERY**	Taxmans Wine	Jungle Telegraph
1984	MANCHESTER R & B Various		Clardan
1985	PHIL GUY	It's a Real Mutha	JSP
1986	KASHMIR	Stay Calm	MrsAckroyd
1986	**NORMAN BEAKER BAND**	**Bought in the Act**	Clardan

157

1987	PHIL GUY	I once was a Gambler	JSP
1988	**NORMAN BEAKER BAND**	Modern Days Lonely Night	JSP

1988	PAUL JONES US GUESTS BBC	Vol 1	JSP
1988	CAREY BELL	Harpslinger	JSP
1998	PAUL JONES US GUESTS	Vol 2	JSP
1988	UP JUMPED THE BLUES	Various	Clardan
1989	**NORMAN BEAKER BAND**	**Into The Blues**	JSP
1994	CAREY BELL	Harpmaster	JSP
1994	PAUL JONES US GUESTS	BBC Vol 3	JSP
1994	TIM WHEATER	Timeless	Image
1994	BURNLEY BLUES FESTIVAL	Vol 1	JSP
1995	PHIL GUY	Breaking out on Top	JSP
1995	CHRIS FARLOWE	Lonesome Road	Indigo
1995	ALEXIS KORNER MEMORIAL	Vol 1	Indigo
1995	ALEXIS KORNER MEMORIAL	Vol 2	Indigo
1995	ALEXIS KORNER MEMORIAL	Vol 3	Indigo
1995	VARIOUS	No Free Rides	JSP
1995	NOTHIN' BUT THE BLUES	Various	JSP
1995	THIS IS BLUES	Sampler	Indigo
1996	RUBY TURNER	Guilty	Indigo
1996	MICK ABRAHAMS	Micks Back	Indigo
1996	DETONATORS	Sneaking Around	Indigo
1997	VARIOUS	Chicago Blues	JSP
1997	CONFESSIN' THE BLUES	Various	Indigo
1997	YOUNG MANS BLUES	Various	JSP
1997	INDIGO BLUESCOLLECTION	Vol 2	Indigo
1998	**NORMAN BEAKER**	**The Older I get the Better I was**	Citadel
1998	LOUISIANA RED	Blues Spectrum	JSP
1999	VARIOUS	Roadhouse Blues	Delta
2000	CHRIS FARLOWE	Glory Bound	Delicious
2000	VARIOUS	Blues Here and There	Crimson
2001	RUBY TURNER	Beatles Blues	Indigo
2002	CHRIS FARLOWE	The Voice	Cloud 9
2002	**NORMAN BEAKER BAND**	**Who's he calling me him**	Delicious
2002	ROCKIN' SIDNEY	I'm your Man	JSP
2003	CHRIS FARLOWE	Farlowe That	Delicious
2003	MILLER ANDERSON	Bluesheart	CherryRed
2003	BUXTON 95 (box set)	Alexis Korner Memorial	Indigo
2004	CHRIS FARLOWE	Rock and Roll Soldier	Delicious
2005	RUBY TURNER	Suspicious Again	Sanctuary
2005	CHRIS FARLOWE	Hungary for the Blues	Delicious
2005	VARIOUS	15 Years Live at Charleys	Mint
2005	THE FIRST FIVE YEARS	Various	Ripley

2006	CHRIS FARLOWE	At Rockpalast	InAkustik
2007	VARIOUS	Guitar Don't Lie	Wallbreaker
2008	JAMES BOOKER	Manchester 77	Document
2009	CLIFF BENNETT	Nearly Retired	Wienerworld
2010	LARRY GARNER	Live at the Tivoi	JNR
2013	LARRY GARNER	**Goodnight in Vienna**	JNR
2014	CHRIS FARLOWE	Collectors Premium	
2014	DEEPLY VALE FESTIVAL	Various	Ozit
2015	**NORMAN BEAKER TRIO**	**Live in Belgrade**	JNR
2016	MILLER ANDERSON	Bluesheart / Chameleon	
2016	REBECCA DOWNES	Believe	MadHat
2018	JOHN PRICE / NORMAN BEAKER	**Between the Lines**	JNR
2018	**NORMAN BEAKER BAND**	**We see us Later**	JNR
2018	LOUISIANA SWAMP BLUES	Vol 2	Wolf
2020	SUNNYSIDERS	The Bridge	Dancing Bear
2020	FENTON ROBINSON	Out of Chicago	JSP

2020	AL ROSS & THE PLANETS	Blue Crystal	Wienerworld
2020	**NORMAN BEAKER**	**Running Down the Clock**	Klock
2022	CRASH HELMUTS	Crash Course	Wienerworld

VIDEOS

1997	HERBIE GOINS/ JOHNNY MARS -	9TH BURNLEY BLUES FES	JSP
1998	JACK BRUCE	ECO ROCK FESTIVAL	Umbrella
2006	CHRIS FARLOWE / NORMAN BEAKER -	GASTROBLUES FESTIVAL	Biem Arts
2006	CHRIS FARLOWE	ROCKPALAST	Inakustik

BOOKS

1989	THE SAFEST PLACE IN THE WORLD	*DICK HECKSTALL- SMITH*	
1995	BLUES IN BRITAIN	*BOB BRUNNING*	Blandford
1996	ALEXIS KORNER BIOGRAPHY	*HARRY SHAPIRO*	Bloomsbury
2005	JACK (BRUCE)	STEVEN MYATT	Aureus
2015	MADE IN THE NORTH	*PAUL WOLFGANG WEBSTER*	
2017	DIRTY STOP OUTS MANCHESTER	*RIKKI WRIGHT*	Acmretro
2010	JACK BRUCE COMPOSING HIMSELF -	*HARRY SHAPIRO*	Jawbone

Printed in Great Britain
by Amazon

83836392R00098